FRIENDS ON THE WATER

Fly Fishing in Good Company

FRIENDS ON THE WATER

Fly Fishing in Good Company

Photographs by R. Valentine Atkinson

Stewart, Tabori & Chang • New York

Foreword

Val Atkinson has fly fished as many places on the planet as anyone—ever. Along the way he has elegantly captured the places, fish, and people encountered with his camera . . . moments large and small.

Such is the human experience that large events in our lives are often overshadowed by small moments. I experienced this firsthand in various World War II engagements. We saw many horrors and unpleasant things, but those are not what I remember. Instead, it's the interesting, off-beat, or comical episodes—and the camaraderie—that cause me to reflect and smile.

So it is with fly fishing. Of course we all remember the biggest fish we ever caught, but the sport of fly fishing keeps us coming back for other reasons—perhaps most of all for the companionship of cherished friends and the funny and memorable things that happen when we're together. The fly fishermen who get the most from the sport understand that it is sharing experiences with our comrades—not merely catching fish—that makes fly fishing such a wonderful pastime.

Because of his warm and unassuming personality, people gravitate to Val. The number of his fly-fishing friends is legion. In this book Val has asked some of his friends to contribute their favorite memories of fly-fishing companionship. These memories—from the humorous to the poignant—are wonderfully complemented by Val's superb photography.

Anyone who's ever taught a son or daughter to read a hatch, laughed at a friend's telling of a favorite fishing tale, or wondered at the grace of a stranger's cast will appreciate the warmth and spirit of *Friends on the Water*. It's a book to sit back and enjoy—and then share again with others.

—Lefty Kreh

Introduction

The world of fly fishing often transports the angler into a magical kingdom. Passionate fly fishers travel to some of the most beautiful and serene places on earth: crystal-clear mountain streams filled with snow-melted waters; meadow spring creeks meandering through pastoral valleys; the wilderness lakes and ponds of the Great North Woods; saltwater flats teeming with new and unusual curiosities set against tropical landscapes of white sand beaches and coconut palms.

To be immersed in these wonderful places is to experience a humbling and spiritual connection with Mother Nature. And sharing these treasured moments with good friends and family elevates them to the sublime. Whether we're stalking bonefish in the Bahamas, attempting to match the hatch on a big Western river, traversing a trail to some distant water, or just relaxing around a campfire with a glass of good cheer, these are shared memories that will last a lifetime.

I've been truly fortunate to spend the last thirty years traveling on assignment to the world's most spectacular locations with camera and fly rod in hand, capturing these places and shared angling experiences on film.

In this book, *Friends on the Water*, I've attempted to do something unique. I've assembled images that I believe will illustrate my enthusiasm for wild and romantic places, as well as the friends and acquaintances who have shared them with me. Accompanying my photographs are many of my favorite stories—warm, poignant, and often funny writings about fishing with companions, whether they are husbands or wives, sons or daughters, fishing guides or dogs. These special pieces are written by notable fishermen— Norman Maclean, Ernie Schwiebert, Nick Lyons, Tom McGuane, Zane Grey, Margot Page, and many others—about their experiences of companionship on the water.

We all need to cherish, respect, and protect what wilderness remains and actively resist the greed that threatens these sanctuaries. If we're successful, our grandchildren will one day find them as lovely and pristine as they appear here, and they too will have the warm memory of sharing nature and fishing with their friends and companions.

Here's to truth, adventure, and passion.

R. Valentine Atkinson

Neither of us said a word,
which is the kind of thing that can happen with old fishing partners:
The fat may be in the fire, but there's no need for discussion.

—John Gierach, *The View from Rat Lake*

The Fishing Camp by Tully Stroud

Fishermen do many odd things in the name of having fun. Prominent among these peculiar activities is the fishing trip to a location where living conditions give new meaning to the word squalor. And great premiums are usually paid for the privilege of forsaking even the most elementary of creature comforts.

These dedicated, but arguably deranged, trout chasers are enjoying a drying out period after six straight days of rain in the Alaskan bush. The weather posed no obstacle to the fishing, of course, but it definitely put a damper on campfires. Worse, a mess tent with more holes than canvas made evening poker games impossible.

All this may not sound serious, but it strikes a blow to the very essence of a fishing trip. After the last cast is made and darkness forces a retreat to the fire, the sport continues. More fish are hooked and lost over the beers and the card games than are ever encountered in the streams. Not because fishermen are liars, but because every strike is relived and every pool refished until the imagination runs amuck.

Fishing without the camaraderie of the camp is like a river without fish—the water's there, but the heart and soul are missing.

Always a Friend by Jerry Darkes

Michael A. Bennett and I fished for trout, but we never referred to ourselves as trout fishermen. We were fly fishermen and we fished for everything we could. From the Great Lakes, to Key West, to the Bahamas and more, anything with fins was regarded as fair game. We accumulated a long list of fly-caught species. We even joked about the "trout fags" who turned up their noses at our excitement about enticing a channel catfish, quillback, or other oddball to hit a fly. Hell, one of our favorite catches ever was a giant bullfrog that jumped a deer hair popper. Purist fly fishers we were not, fun we had.

Michael is gone now, but in thinking about him, we first met trout fishing and my final time on the water with him was trout fishing. In spite of all our wandering, trout fishing was the beginning and end, our alpha and omega. Oddly, though, I can probably count on my fingers the days we

spent on a trout stream. From our base in northern Ohio, real trout fishing with hatches and everything was several hours away. Steelhead, bass, and bluegill took up our local efforts.

I first met Michael when he was a student in a "Getting Started in Fly Fishing" class I was teaching. Always an avid sportsman, he did not start fly fishing until he turned fifty. We left the weekend class like we had been friends for life and our journey started.

Michael contacted me several times afterwards to guide himself and a friend, John Gillette. We fished in western Pennsylvania and one of his first real trout stream experiences was hitting the start of the sulphur hatch on Oil Creek. Lots of bugs, rising trout, and a warm day in May provided the perfect start for a beginning angler.

The following fall I suggested giving steelhead a try. This was back when Ohio and

Pennsylvania's Lake Erie tributaries were still a secret and had not yet earned the "Steelhead Alley" monicker. One fish was all it took and Michael discovered what would ultimately define his fly-fishing career.

After that first experience, Michael spent the fall, winter, and following spring chasing steelhead every spare moment he got. He called after every trip to share his success and analyze his failures. We started fishing together on a regular basis and I was amazed at how fast his fly-fishing knowledge and skill began to accumulate. He was a practicing psychologist and I often joked he consider counseling for his obsessive behavior.

A few years ago after a trip to the Yellowstone area Michael started complaining of all kinds of strange pains and feeling tired all the time. He was tested for Lyme's disease, but nothing positive ever showed. That fall he started having to cancel guide trips. Additional testing indicated a possible bleeding ulcer. With him not feeling up to walking a stream, Michael and I opted to spend a few hours chasing trout at one of the private clubs near Castalia, Ohio. On the ride up we reminisced about past adventures and talked about an upcoming trip to the Bahamas the following spring.

That trip was the last time Michael and I got to fish together. Shortly afterwards the doctors finally got to the bottom of his problem. He was diagnosed with inoperable stomach cancer that had spread to his lymph nodes, a death sentence with an estimated six months to live. He found out on New Year's Eve day.

Over the next months Michael struggled with his illness and his condition deteriorated as predicted. We watched helplessly, trying to figure out some way to counsel our friend who had always been there to counsel us. We had scheduled a trip to the Bahamas before we were aware of his illness and Michael still hoped to make that trip. We knew he would not be able to travel again and we canceled.

The last time I saw Michael we talked and he did not feel cheated or short-changed. He said he had done and accomplished more in his life than he ever expected and there is not much more any of us can really ask for. He said he was being cremated and was asking several of us to take portions of his ashes to several of his favorite fishing places. That way he could get us on one final fishing trip together.

Michael passed away peacefully on a sunny May afternoon almost three years ago to the day I am writing this. He was at home surrounded by family. I am guessing that the sulphurs had just started hatching on Oil Creek like the first time he fished there.

His long-time friend John Gillette spread a part of Michael's ashes on a lake up in Ontario where Michael fished with his father and still tried to get to for a few days every year. We had an informal ceremony with family and friends at a favorite steelhead pool on Pennsylvania's Elk Creek. Both John and I got the chore to take Michael to a picturesque bonefish flat on Long Island. We each caught a fish on the flat and toasted Michael's memory with a cold Kalik.

I was back at Michael's Flat about a year later. When we approached the small island where we had spread Michael's ashes, I saw a group of silver tails happily moving through the shallows. It was good to know my old friend was still there, looking out for me.

{excerpt}

Big Fish by Nick Lyons

From where I stood I did not always see the fly alight on the slate surface of the water, and now and then I'd pour myself another lemonade or fuss with my reel or line. I felt very contented. I had caught a couple of remarkable fish and that, thank you, had been quite enough. But I was facing the river and whenever I looked up I saw it and Herb and watched until whatever little drama was being played was done. I was looking up when I saw a fish rise twice, then—with a wake—drift off to the right. Then it came back and took four or five PMDs. Herb watched, tense now, waiting to cast. I wondered why he was waiting so long. Did he want the fish to get good and confident? It was clearly a very big fish, but there were a lot of big fish in this pool and it was quite impossible to tell from the delicate rise and the wake quite how large this one might be.

For a few moments the feeding stopped. Then I saw the slight bulge and dimple of the fish, about seventy-five feet out, to the right, and then I saw Herb's rapid cast.

I saw his bright yellow parachute alight four or five feet up from where the water had pinched a moment before. The cast, with only one false

cast far to the left, had been exactly on target. The rumpled leader started to straighten, the fly moved ever so slowly on a current you could not see, and I felt my heart leaning out into the water, straining after the fly—my breath slightly irregular—wanting to coax the fish into taking.

That moment was more than six years ago and memory, for me, about fishing, always mingles with fantasy and dream. But this memory is too sharply etched not to have been real.

I remember the long length of line going back and then forward, and then shooting to a distance of perhaps seventy feet. I remember the #17 Pale Morning Dun parachute alighting with a final little somersault of the leader and then picking up what there was of current and floating slowly downstream. I remember the expectation and the wait. And I remember with perfect clarity—when I run the entire scene out in my mind, in sequence—the slight pinch and bulge of the flat surface . . . and then the sudden, immense, electric rush of force.

The trout took Herb's fly lightly and did not move off unperturbed by the prick, like the books say. The fish zoomed off like a bonefish—hard and fast and far, in a straight line, like any wild thing

held; and then, two hundred feet up the long pool, it leaped once, erupting, exploding, splattering the air with bubbles and silver splashes of water.

"Bigger than I thought," Herb said.

He stood up now, intent, looking upstream.

"Parachute?" I asked.

Herb nodded.

I worried about the size of his leader point and asked: "Six-X?"

He nodded again.

After the jump the fish settled down to doing what a truly big fish is supposed to do. It moved off heavily, steadily, heading for the uppermost part of the pool, where the river pinched through the last narrow sections of land and broadened and slowed.

The fish was clearly larger—by a great measure —than the two fish I'd taken. Quite how large it was I could not tell. The fish was now well into the backing, perhaps three hundred feet upstream, and all you could see was the long expanse of buck-skin fly line and then the smaller white backing, and at the far end a steady surge of water, as if a foul-hooked muskrat or a beaver or an otter was burrowing just beneath the surface. There was simply no way that this fish would not break off.

Herb's leader was decisive. He could not have held the fish without it. For with all that line out, and the fish making sudden moves to the left or right, the 6X leader would surely otherwise have broken. But it did not. The fish veered off toward the far bank and the tippet held. The fish slashed at the surface and I thought that surely now it was gone; but the line was still taut when the com-motion stopped. The great trout came up twice more—hugely, splattering water high, shaking, then crashing back down—with ninety feet of fly line and 280 feet of backing between it and the fly rod, and the fish was still on, and heading still father upstream, around the bend.

You could not begin to pressure such a fish on such tackle yet, but you could stay with it, subtly —lean into it, drop your rod tip when it jumped, lower the rod (as Vince Marinaro advised) when the fish ran, so the line came directly off a finely tuned reel, with less friction. With abrupt, deft, athletic movements, Herb managed it all.

But then I saw him fumble with his reel and lean forward awkwardly, his rod extended as far as he could extend it in front of him. Something had happened. Was the line tangled? Surely he'd lose the fish now.

The bottom of the pool here was muddy and pocked with muskrat holes. It would be treacherous to wade toward the fish, and to get out of the pool and walk up the brushy, irregular bank could be fatal to the fight in a dozen ways. No, he had to stay in the water, where he was, in that one spot, and he had to manage the fish from that fixed position where he stood. There were no other options, no other ways to save what was becoming a desperate situation.

I did not have to stay so far from the action so I had walked to a high bank upstream where I'd have a better chance to see the great trout. I trotted back now to see if I could help Herb with whatever problem he had. The problem was this: the fish had taken the last foot of backing and for a moment—fumbling with the reel, leaning forward —Herb was trying to reach out and secure another foot or two of line before the gigantic fish broke off, which surely it would do. The fish was at the very end of the backing and sort of wallowing there, not pressing forward, finally tired perhaps, after the run, the shaking, the acrobatics. The fish could not be pressured but perhaps it could be urged, and Herb leaned his rod back a bit, then dropped

it and reeled, to regain another foot or so of line. But the line would not come back onto the spool; tied loosely, with a slip knot—the only carelessness in Herb's rig, or perhaps not—the line was circling the spool without coming back into it. With the fish moving slightly toward him now, the line threatened to go slack.

Herb's fingers, fussing with the circling line, grew frantic for a moment.

Still leaning forward, he had to tighten the knot with his free fingers and coax line back onto the reel.

Well, that's it, I thought. A fly line and one hundred yards of backing hadn't been enough to hold this fish. If the great fish made a sudden move now, Herb would lose it for sure.

But despite the slack and the fumbling, the fish was still on.

Foot by foot Herb urged the gigantic thing back toward him, regaining half, then three-quarters of the backing as the fish turned and headed heavily, at an angle, downstream. There was no urgency in its movements now; the fish was subdued, worn, if not yet quite beaten. It could be led without being forced. The process—now done by inches— required immense patience.

Back on the high bank I kept my eyes flicking from fisherman to fish. In ten minutes the trout was back onto the reel and I knew that it would only take a few more minutes before Herb had it at his side and would be reaching down to release it. I'd seen him handle the endgame flawlessly dozens of times.

The fish was near the surface now, canted to one side slightly, not twenty feet from me, and I could look down and see it with absolute clarity. I can see it still, all these years later. The trout was a full foot longer than the two I'd caught, thicker by far, more than double their weight. And it was nearly beaten. I have seen larger trout come from lakes, on leaders the size of cables; steelhead are larger, even stronger; and this was fully the size of a dozen Atlantic salmon I'd seen. Why did this fish seem then—and why does it still seem—the most prodigious trout I'd ever seen? Surely the light tackle—not an affectation but a necessity for luring such a fish—and the relative size of the fish to this type of fishing played their roles. But a two-pound bluegill, even a giant of its species, is still only two pounds of bluegill, a piker. This fish was a monster.

"It's heading toward the weeds," Herb said flatly. "Can't put more pressure on."

The big head came half up out of the water and shook once, and the leader held, and Herb coaxed it slightly, firmly, away from the weeds. I felt quite sure he'd keep the great trout out of the weedbed. I felt sure he'd take it now, with only thirty or forty feet of line out.

And then the fish went a couple of feet off to the right, into the region of the weeds, and was off—and I felt then, and feel now, years later, as you must feel reading this, as all of us feel at such moments—as if I'd lost a part of myself and would forever be searching for it.

Herb reeled in quickly, checked the end of his leader, and found that the #17 golden fly had neither broken off nor bent straight, but simply pulled free. "Didn't break him off," he said. He smiled, shook his head, and said mildly, "That was a very big fish, Nick."

Now, so long afterward, I can forgive him his insouciance: a man who could fight a fish so well and lose it with so little trauma had to have caught a dozen that size.

I'd have punched myself silly.

[excerpt]

Fishin' Food by Alan Liere

Having recently experimented with a low-carb diet during which I subsisted on air chips and ice wraps, I was delighted to see the winter fishing season begin.

Winter fly fishing is not at all like summer fly fishing. While engaged in summer fishing, it is easy to begin feeling guilty about the number of calories being consumed between casts because the evidence of your overindulgence is pooching up over the top of your hip boots like a great, white water balloon.

Each time I take off my shirt to catch a few summer angling rays just before dropping a #16 Yellow Sally atop a sulking Savage River rainbow, I am reminded that while Mountain Dew and potato chips are the essence of warm-weather fishing, they aren't doing much for my figure.

It's not something I swell on, as I long ago surrendered my Mr. Universe fantasy in favor of staying within fifty pounds of my "perfect weight." Late in the summer, however, I sometimes think about the shape I'm in when I notice the sun is not tanning all parts of my belly equally. It seems to me I look rather like a tiger, with white stripes between the rolls of golden excess.

Winter fishing is much better if you view eating as part of the total experience. On a winter fishing expedition, one can get rid of all sorts of leftover holiday junk and not feel guilty about it, primarily because you don't notice its effects with all that bulky clothing on. Also, it is easier to justify overeating when the weather is cold, for who's to say when you might have to subsist on accumulated fat reserves?

My friend Mike Sweeney is my favorite person to winter fish with. Mike thinks a balanced meal is one where you have equal portions of Twinkies and potato chips. On our frequent trips, I sometimes have to remind him to "pack light" because of space limitations in the car. If this means leaving his rod, reel, and fly box at home, so be it, but Mike is never without a cooler stuffed with worthless calories: he doesn't bring candy bars; he brings candy stores. Chocolate peanut clusters,

bags of M&Ms, Little Debbie Oatmeal Creme Pies —take your pick. Better yet, take lots of each. For a person like me who, as a child, could buy sweets only once a week on allowance day, Mike is The Candy Man.

Usually, I suppose as a joke, Mike's cooler also holds apples or a bag of yuppie carrots, but I suspect he recycles these. Apples do not have an "eat by" date, and when they are wrinkled and starting to turn brown, I've got a pretty good idea they are the same props I saw on the last trip.

Sometimes Mike and I never get around to catching fish. With a crackling fire heating up the landscape and the rods propped against a tree, we sometimes just sit around cultivating a sugar high, wondering what the poor folks are doing. For variety we add Cheetos or Doritos to our diet, but these are washed down with hot chocolate, and I never, ever talk about cholesterol or clogged arteries unless Mike is working on the last Krispy Kreme and I want a bite.

Soon enough, it will be spring and I'll have to shed my winter chest waders and don my light summer hip boots. Oh, Mike and I will still over-indulge on grease and sugar then, but I imagine we'll sometimes feel bad about what we're doing to our bodies.

In the meantime, I'm going to pack on a few guiltless pounds. You never can tell when you'll be snowbound.

A Lab's Life by Greg Thomas

I'm on Night One of a five-day trip to Idaho's Clearwater River, an attempt to land and release as many of those big, meaty, B-run steelhead as is humanly possible. But it's four o'clock in a narrow mountain canyon and, to my surprise, already dark. Suddenly, I have no idea what I'll do during the fourteen hours before daylight returns, confined to the back of the truck with two spoiled Labrador retrievers.

Already, I've tied enough egg-sucking leeches and conehead muddlers to supply an army, and the twenty-mile run to the bars in Orofino represents a dangerous journey. I place a Coleman stove on the tailgate, oil a pan, and construct a monumental meat patty before a captive audience. Snow falls in heavy, wet, saturating flakes. The temperature falls from thirty-five to fifteen in less than an hour.

"It's going to be fun tomorrow," I tell Moose and Shadow. I'm three bits away from completing the meal when I get the chills and retrieve a stocking hat from the cab. I return to find the tailgate licked clean, my High Life knocked to the ground. I should have known. Moose once opened a cooler and ate five Hungarian partridge—every wing, foot, head, beak, and bone. Shadow stole sixty-two strips of deer jerky off a counter.

"Who ate my burger?" I yell. "Bad dogs!" they look innocent as larks. Moose's left eyebrow raises, the right falls in unison. I interrogate him and he diverts eyes. Shadow moans and inches her thirteen-year-old frame onto the nest I've created—two cedar-chip beds, a foam pad, and a down sleeping bag. It's an act. She shares equal blame. A hidden camera would have recorded a dead-heat.

Her stomach growls, the grease taking effect.

I stash the stove and grimy pan under the truck and climb in with the hounds. I kill the dome light and retreat to my down bag. It's dark as a cave. The dogs sense we're in for the long haul. They know the routine as well as I do. There are rustling noises, motion, and Shadow's cold snout against my cheek. Moose's 115 pounds rises, then falls hard against my hip, pinning me against the wheel well. I place hands against cold steel and leverage my ass to regain a portion of the sleeping pad. It's a turf war that will last all night.

Now it's nine and I can't begin to sleep; I can't stop thinking about a steelhead hooked earlier that day, visualizing its determined run to the far bank, its impossible six jumps, its crimson gillplates. I rise, turn on the light, and greet the Old Crow. I fill half a coffee mug. It's harsh and warm. I pour another, acknowledge the shivering dogs, and recall a wicked-cold New Year's Day when I drove from Seattle to Montana, across ice-covered roads, stopping at bars to check the bowl games. I was headed to the Gallatin. I ran out of gas near Drummond, which was a good thing because I'd already declared myself a threat to society. The temperature was minus-twenty and I didn't have a sleeping bag. I put on every item of clothing I had, climbed into a pair of 5MM neoprenes and lay down in the bed of the truck with Shadow in my arms and Moose on my head. I woke up covered in death frost and dog hair.

The Old Crow is so good I pour another. Now, feeling giddy, I'm willing to forgive. Shadow crawls headfirst down my sleeping bag and I offer Moose a Vienna sausage. Who cares about sleep and smelling like a wet Lab? We've got four more days and the steelhead are in.

Well, I'm ——! by G. E. M. Skues

Mr. Theodore Castwell, having devoted a long, strenuous, and not unenjoyable life to hunting to their doom innumerable salmon, trout, and grayling in many quarters of the globe, and having gained much credit among his fellows for his many ingenious improvements in rods, flies, and tackle employed for that end, in the fullness of time died and was taken to his own place.

St. Peter looked up from a draft balance sheet at the entry of the attendant angel.

"A gentleman giving the name of Castwell. Says he is a fisherman, your Holiness, and has 'Fly-fishers' Club, London,' on his card."

"Hm-hm," says St. Peter. "Show him in."

Mr. Castwell entered cheerfully and offered a cordial right hand to St. Peter.

"As a brother of the angle——" he began.

"Hm-hm," said St. Peter.

"I am sure I shall not appeal to you in vain for special consideration in connection with the quarters to be assigned to me here."

"Hm-hm," said St. Peter. "I have been looking at your account from below."

"Nothing wrong with it, I hope," said Mr. Castwell.

"Hm-hm," said St. Peter. "I have seen worse. What sort of quarters would you like?"

"Well," said Mr. Castwell. "Do you think you could manage something in the way of a country cottage of the Test Valley type, with modern conveniences and, say, three-quarters of a mile of one of those pleasant chalk streams, clear as crystal, which proceed from out the throne, attached?"

"Why, yes," said St. Peter. "I think we can manage that for you. Then what about your gear? You must have left your fly rods and tackle down below. I see you prefer a light split cane of nine foot or so, with appropriate fittings. I will indent upon the Works Department for what you require, including a supply of flies. I think you will approve of our dressers' productions. Then you will want a keeper to attend you."

"Thanks awfully, your Holiness," said Mr. Castwell. "That will be first-rate. To tell you the truth, from the Revelations I read, I was inclined to fear that I might be just a teeny-weeny bit bored in heaven."

"In H—hm-hm," said St. Peter, checking himself.

It was not long before Mr. Castwell found himself alongside an enchantingly beautiful clear chalk stream, some fifteen yards wide, swarming with fine trout feeding greedily; and presently the attendant angel assigned to him had handed him the daintiest, most exquisite, light split cane rod conceivable—perfectly balanced with reel and line—with a beautifully damped tapered cast of incredible fitness and strength—and a box of flies of such marvelous trying as to be almost mistakable for the natural insects they were to simulate.

Mr. Castwell scooped up a natural fly from the water, matched it perfectly from the fly box, and knelt down to cast to a riser putting up just under a tussock ten yards or so above him. The fly hit like gossamer, six inches above the last ring; and next moment the rod was making the curve of beauty. Presently, after an exciting battle, the keeper netted out a beauty of about two and a half pounds.

"Heavens!" cried Mr. Castwell. "This is something like."

"I am sure his Holiness will be pleased to hear it," said the keeper.

Mr. Castwell prepared to move upstream to the next riser when he became aware that another trout had taken up the position of that which he had just landed, and was rising. "Just look at that," he said, dropping instantaneously to his knee and drawing off some line. A moment later an accurate fly fell just above the neb of the fish, and instantly Mr. Castwell engaged in battle with another lusty fish. All went well, and presently the landing net received its two and a half pounds.

"A very pretty brace," said Mr. Castwell, preparing to move on to the next of the string of busy nebs which he had observed putting up round the bend. As he approached the tussock, however, he became aware that the place from which he had just extracted so satisfactory a brace was already occupied by another busy feeder.

"Well, I'm damned!" cried Mr. Castwell. "Do you see that?"

"Yes, sir," said the keeper. . .

Mr. Castwell turned joyfully to approach the next riser round the bend. Judge, however, his surprise to find that once more the pit beneath the tussock was occupied by a rising trout, apparently of much the same size as the others.

"Heavens!" exclaimed Mr. Castwell. "Was there ever anything like it?"

"No, sir," said the keeper.

"Look here," said he to the keeper, "I think I really must give this chap a miss and pass on to the next."

"Sorry! It can't be done, sir. His Holiness would not like it."

"Well, if that's really so," said Mr. Castwell, and knelt reluctantly to his task.

Several hours later he was still casting to the same tussock.

"How long is this confounded rise going to last?" inquired Mr. Castwell. "I suppose it will stop soon?"

"No, sir," said the keeper.

"What, isn't there a slack hour in the afternoon?"

"No afternoon, sir."

"What? Then what about the evening rise?"

"No evening, sir," said the keeper.

"Well, I shall knock off now. I must have had about thirty brace from that corner."

"Beg pardon, sir, but his Holiness would not like that."

"What?" said Mr. Castwell. "Mayn't I even stop at night?"

"No night here, sir," said the keeper.

"Then do you mean that I have got to go on catching these damned two and a half pounders at this corner for ever and ever?"

The keeper nodded.

"Hell!" said Mr. Castwell.

"Yes," said his keeper.

Fishing with Ghosts by Bob White

Fishing at the Boca is as much of a social event as a private one, and there are certain, specific places where one stands to cast. A fisherman works the water in front of him methodically for fifteen to twenty minutes and moves to the next position, relinquishing the spot to the next angler who follows. There are four or five such stations before the "Fool's Pool," and the big bend. The lead position is one of respect, and the most senior fisherman in the group is usually asked to begin. In this case, our clients were the most important and they were asked to start.

Jorge read my mind as he watched my gaze drift from the river to my unopened rod case.

"Why don't you follow, Señor Blanco?" he offered. "There's not much guiding to be done here today."

I'd been waiting for this opportunity the entire season, and my rod was strung up in record time. I was tying on some fresh tippet, while Jorge led the others to the water, suggesting that they use a large, dark fly.

Peter and Richard fished through the sequence twice, very quickly, before Jorge joined them for a third. Jorge is a very thoughtful fisherman, who knows the value of fishing such a place in a slow and methodical rhythm, and his two clients were finished long before he'd reached the second position. I suspected that he would give much to have another chance at the big fish he lost in 1976.

As a sign of respect, I waited until he was at the third position before I started. I tested the strength of my knots and the sharpness of the hook, stripped line from my reel, took a deep breath, and began false casting until my timing smoothed out, and made that first long cast. I remember feeling then, like I feel now, when I buy a lottery ticket. Don't tell me about the odds . . . I just KNOW that this is the time that I'll hit it big.

The first cast hit the water and started to swing

in the current as the sinking tip pulled the big, black maribou muddler under the surface and through the current. I saw in my mind's eye what I had dreamed might happen. As the line straightened out at the end of the swing, I tensed . . . and stripped it back . . . and felt exactly the same way as when my lottery ticket doesn't win: this next time just HAS TO BE THE ONE!

I paced myself to Jorge, casting as he did, and letting the fly swing its entire arch before starting a retrieve. Soon, the rhythm of our casting was the same and neither of us watched the other, lost in our own dreams and memories. We both fished through the stations without a touch and Jorge wisely decided that it was more important to attend to his customers and catch up with old friends than to chase ghosts.

"You go ahead, Bob, fish it through again. These guys are all having a good time . . . and I'll open some bottles of tinto."

I walked back to the lake as Jorge went to the truck for wine. Someone added wood to the fire and a shower of sparks towered into the darkening sky and drifted off, disappearing before the wind.

By the time I'd reached the second station, the sound of the waves, the wind, and the repetitiveness of the casting had mesmerized me. I was thinking about ghosts and what Jorge had said when it happened. The line came tight and my rod bent double, nearly hitting the water. Line hissed through my fingers and arched out into the lake across the crests of the growing waves. The fish had taken all of the slack and was on the reel as he powered out into the depths of the big lake. The reel screamed and I was applying as much pressure as I dared when the big brown jumped. He cleared the water and seemed to hang there for

seconds before landing slab-sided, in a trough, between two waves.

A cheer erupted from behind me as the fish jumped a second time, and a third. I was just beginning to feel in control of the situation when the line went sickeningly slack, and the crowd, now gathered at the water's edge, collectively moaned like a mortally wounded beast. As my heart sank, the fish rocketed from the waves again . . . and again . . . and one last time! Everyone was cheering—this time for the fish—and I bowed my head in defeat, like a tragic character in an apocalyptic opera.

The crowd called out their condolences as they drifted back to the fire, inviting me to share some wine and tell them my story . . . but I couldn't. I felt like someone who, after years of trying, finally won the lottery, and then lost the winning ticket. It was too painful to relive so soon. I thought of Jorge and his big fish and knew that he'd understand.

I moved downstream to the next station, focused my energies as best I could, and prayed to the fish god for just one more chance. On my second cast, as the fly swung deeply through a small pool in the center of the river, a good fish took and ran downstream, through a field of boulders and toward the depths of the "Fool's Pool." I got my rod tip high and threaded my way downstream to the lip of the big pool. The fish circled there, unsure if it should go further downstream or make a break, back upriver, for the safety of the lake. I empathized with its dilemma, and understood its choice to stay there and bide its time—after all, there is a certain sense of safety in indecision. How many times had I done the same thing, I wondered?

I wore the fish out carefully and gradually, her frantic efforts into the green depths of the pool growing less and less determined. Finally, after she'd already spent the energy necessary to escape, she tried gaining the safety of the lake. Again, I understood her situation, and felt insight into my own life through her struggle. Failing in her attempt to reach the lake, she decided on an escape downriver. As she turned and ran past me, I swung my rod low and left, using her momentum, and turned her as she neared the shore.

Defeated, she lay on her side, there in the shallow water, her eyes rolled down—always focused on the world where she belonged.

"Great fish!" said Prince Radziwill, as he grasped her through her gills and lifted her as a trophy for all to see. "Congratulations."

"No!" I screamed, taking her back from him and walking her out into the current. "God damn it!" I thought, as I watched a slight trace of blood pumping through her gills. I knew from experience that once a fish was bleeding from its gills, it was unlikely to survive its release. I revived her as best I could, and let her slip from my hands. She swam upstream toward the lake and an uncertain future.

"I'm so sorry," I said, turning to the Prince. "I meant no offense. I was just taken with the moment . . . please forgive my outburst."

"I understand," he said. "The times have changed . . . and I think for the best. Please forgive me. I was also taken with the moment. Would you like some wine?"

But I didn't stop and join the others after releasing the brown. I stood on the lip of the "Fool's Pool" and hooked a third big fish. I played it as best I could, determined to do everything right, but the big male threw the hook on its second jump and sulked in plain view until dark. Upon inspecting the fly, I found that I'd fractured the hook on a low back-cast. It was broken at the bend, but there was still a point to it. The crowd, gathered there before the river, at the edge of night, cheered for the both of us.

A few days later, I sat on an airliner as it traveled north along the spine of the Andes, and watched the setting sun. There was much to think about . . . much I wanted to remember, and more that I was afraid to forget.

"There are many ghosts at the Boca," Jorge had said. I wondered about those ghosts. Were they the ghosts of fish or men? Weren't the two really intertwined into one memory, and wasn't that the essence of the ghost? If you fish hard and the fishing

There are many ghosts at the Boca . . .

—JORGE TRUCCO

becomes your life, sooner or later you fish with ghosts . . . and eventually you become one.

Since that first season's end, I've lost many companions to the vagaries of time. Jorge, Donovan, and Bebe have since crossed over . . . friends of mine report having seen them at the Boca. When I fish the Agulukpak, Howard and Jacque are there with me. I never wade the Malleo without thinking of Florencia . . . or the Kinnikinnic without remembering Ed. Finn and Rupert wait patiently for me on the Upper Nushagak. There are others . . . too many others. These days, I rarely fish alone.

{excerpt}

Rocky Riffle on the Rogue River by Zane Grey

These Rogue River steelhead must have had a council before my arrival to decide upon the infinitely various and endless tricks they would play upon me. To be sure, they played a few upon my comrades, but the great majority, and the hopeless ones and the terrible ones, fell to my lot.

During those unforgettable ten days I kept secret and accurate account of what happened to R. C. and the boys. Some of this I saw myself; part of it I learned at the general campfire narratives of the day's experience, and the rest I acquired by a casual and apparently innocent curiosity. . . .

On October 15 we were due in southeastern Oregon, to take a hunt in a new country. I had still several days to fish before we started, and I could prolong the stay a couple of days longer if desirable. R. C. now had eighteen steelhead to his credit, taken on a fly. The boys had added several to their string. And I still cherished unquenchable hopes. Next day I actually caught a steelhead on a fly, so quickly and surprisingly that I scarcely realized it.

I went down the river later than usual, and found Ken and Ed casting from the dry rocks at the head of Rocky Riffle. R. C. was above in midstream. When I rigged up my tackle, I put on an English salmon fly. It was unlike any fly the steelhead had been rising to, and I meant to try it just for contrariness. Wading in fifty feet above Ken, I made a preliminary cast, and let the fly float down.

Tug! Splash! A steelhead hooked himself and leaped, and ran right into the water Ken was fishing. I waded out, ran below, and fought the fish in an eddy, and soon landed it—a fine plump steelhead weighing about four pounds.

"Bingo! Out goes a fly—in comes a fish!" exclaimed Ed. "Say, you're a fast worker!"

Ken cupped his hand and yelled up to R. C. "Hey, Rome, he's busted his streak of bad luck!"

R. C. waved and called back: "Goodnight! Lock the gate!"

I took R. C.'s good-natured slang—an intimation that they would now have to look out for me—as a happy augury for the remaining days. Next day I caught three: a small one, another around four pounds, and the third over five and a half. . . .

{excerpt}

I have learned not to go crazy if I hike for a while
only to find someone in my private water.

—STEVEN J. MEYERS, *SAN JUAN RIVER CHRONICLE*

The Intruder by Robert Traver

It was about noon when I put down my fly rod and sculled the little cedar boat with one hand and ate a sandwich and drank a can of beer with the other, just floating and enjoying the ride down the beautiful broad main Escanaba River. Between times I watched the merest speck of an eagle tacking and endlessly wheeling far up in the cloudless sky. Perhaps he was stalking my sandwich or even, dark thought, stalking me. . . The fishing so far had been poor; the good trout simply weren't rising. I rounded a slow double bend, with high gravel banks on either side, and there stood a lone fisherman—the first person I had seen in hours. He was standing astride a little feeder creek on a gravel point on the left downstream side, fast to a good fish, his glistening rod hooped and straining, the line taut, the leader vibrating and sawing the water, the fish itself boring far down out of sight.

Since I was curious to watch a good battle and anxious not to interfere, I eased the claw anchor over the stern—plop—and the little boat hung there, gurgling and swaying from side to side on the slow deep current. The young fisherman either

did not hear me or, hearing, and being a good one, kept his mind on his work. As I sat watching he shifted the rod to his left hand, shaking out his right wrist as though it were asleep, so I knew then that the fight had been a long one and that this fish was no midget. The young fisherman fumbled in his shirt and produced a cigarette and lighter and lit up, a real cool character. The fish made a sudden long downstream run and the fisherman raced after him, prancing through the water like a yearling buck, gradually coaxing and working him back up to the deeper slow water across from the gravel bar. It was a nice job of handling and I wanted to cheer. Instead I coughed discreetly and he glanced quickly upstream and saw me.

"Hi," he said pleasantly, turning his attention back to his fish.

"Hi," I answered.

"How's luck?" he said, still concentrating.

"Fairish," I said. "But I haven't raised anything quite like you seem to be on to. How you been doin'—otherwise, I mean?"

"Fairish," he said. "This is the third good trout

in this same stretch—all about the same size."

"My, my," I murmured, thinking ruefully of the half-dozen-odd barely legal brook trout frying away in my sun-baked creel. "Guess I've just been out floating over the good spots."

"Pleasant day for a ride, though," he said, frowning intently at his fish.

"Delightful," I said wryly, taking a slow swallow of beer.

"Yep," the assured young fisherman went on, expertly feeding out line as his fish made another downstream sashay. "Yep," he repeated, nicely taking up slack on the retrieve, "that's why I gave up floating this lovely river. Nearly ten years ago, just a kid. Decided then 'twas a hell of a lot more fun fishing a hundred yards of her carefully than taking off on these all-day floating picnics."

I was silent for a while. Then: "I think you've got something there," I said, and I meant it. Of course he was right, and I was simply out joy-riding past the good fishing. I should have brought along a girl or a camera. On this beautiful river if there was no rise a float was simply an enforced if lovely scenic tour. If there was a rise, no decent fisherman ever needed to float. Presto, I now had it all figured out. . . .

"Wanna get by?" the poised young fisherman said, flipping his cigarette into the water.

"I'll wait," I said. "I got all day. My pal isn't meeting me till dark—way down at the old burned logging bridge."

"Hm . . . trust you brought your passport—you really are out on a voyage," he said. "Perhaps you'd better slip by, fella—by the feel of this customer it'll be at least ten-twenty minutes more. Like a smart woman in the mood for play, these big trout don't like to be rushed. C'mon, just bear in sort of close to me, over here, right under London Bridge. It won't bother us at all."

My easy young philosopher evidently didn't want me to see how really big his fish was. But being a fisherman myself I knew, I knew. "All right," I said, lifting the anchor and sculling down over his way and under his throbbing line. "Thanks and good luck."

"Thanks, chum," he said, grinning at me. "Have a nice ride and good luck to you."

"Looks like I'll need it," I said, looking enviously back over my shoulder at his trembling rod tip. "Hey," I said, belatedly remembering my company manners, "want a nice warm can of beer?"

Smiling: "Despite your glowing testimonial, no thanks."

"You're welcome," I said, realizing we were carrying on like a pair of strange diplomats.

"And one more thing, please," he said, raising his voice a little to be heard over the burbling water, still smiling intently at his straining fish. "If you don't mind, please keep this little stretch under your hat—it's been all mine for nearly ten years. It's really something special. No use kidding you—I see you've spotted my bulging creel and I guess by now you've got a fair idea of what I'm on to. And anyway I've got to take a little trip. But I'll be back—soon I hope. In the meantime try to be good to the place. I know it will be good to you."

"Right," I shouted, for by then I had floated nearly around the downstream bend. "Mum's the word." He waved his free hand and then was blotted from view by a tall doomed spruce leaning far down out across the river from a crumbling water-blasted bank. The last thing I saw was the gleaming flash of his rod, the long taut line, the strumming leader. It made a picture I've never forgotten.

[excerpt]

As Was the Father, So Is the Child by Gene Hill

I now have no doubt that for most of my earliest days, the only times I was in any real contact with my father were when we fished together.

Now, when I reflect on those times, I know that my father was troubled by my being with him in the woods. He was a young man, less than thirty, when I was old enough to insist on tagging along. Even when I wasn't wanted, which was often, I would follow him from a distance, knowing that he knew I was there. He would never stop and wait for me, never slow his woodsman's pace to accommodate my young legs. He knew that when the distance between us reached a certain point, I would finally turn around, hurt to the point of tears, and go back home.

When my father was running his trap line, I would shortcut through the woods and wait, silently, for him to come along. I would see him appear through the trees and along a brook, watch him crouch to check a set for mink, and know that he knew I was watching them. As often as not, he

would ignore my being there and go on about his business of checking a set or running it again if it had been sprung. Other times, though, he would be angry and march up to me, pulling a switch from a tree along the way. He would yank me to my feet and bring the switch across my legs. The switch would raise red welts that lasted for days. When he was finished and I picked myself off the ground, I would make my way home and wonder why. And when he got ready to leave a few days later to check his trap line again, I would ask to go and often did—whether I was allowed to or not. I was, I now know, drawn by some ancient pull that I could not resist, offering myself to his silent fury as if I were determined to be sacrificed to something I would never understand. And here I am, ten times older, still drawn by the same ancient pull and still without understanding why.

It was in the summer of my sixth or seventh year that he began to take me fishing. He would

let me go along, not grudgingly but not really willingly either. It was "just along," as you might let a farm dog follow you into the fields, not caring much if it came or not.

The little I thought about it, it didn't seem to me that a father and son had any reason to be friends. I knew he had to care for me, to see that I was fed and clothed and warned away from harm, but I could see no reason, except my wanting him to, for him to like me or even want me at his side.

There were few boys for me to talk to. Even with them our conversations never drifted to the subject of whether we liked or got along with our fathers. Our society dictated that you keep your own counsel. If you were in the mood to ask "strange" questions, you kept your questions to yourself, or asked them in the dark, silently, as an apologetic footnote to nightly prayers.

Fishing was one of the few pleasures my father allowed himself. But even such a simple pleasure as fishing had to be earned. He couldn't simply go fishing in the evening after a hard day's work. The work had to be finished for that day. If there was something that had to be done in the long twilight, it was done first. The garden, which supplied us with much of our food, was a constant chore; it had to be watered by hand-carried pails from the brook that ran close by and constantly weeded—as much for the fact that weeds indicated a level of sloth as anything else.

An evening's fishing was rarely discussed in advance. After supper he would get up from the table and go outside to the shed that held his tackle (an old bamboo plug-casting rod and a tin box with "baits" in it), hand me the bait box, put the oars over his shoulder, and start walking to the lake.

I knew he didn't mind my going with him, because I'd be perched up on the back seat of the rowboat in spite of the fact that the kitchen wood-box hadn't been filled to the top, or there was still a section of lawn not mowed or trimmed. An entire evening could pass, fish or no fish, with no more than a few words being exchanged. Most of the words spoken were directed to me to keep quiet or to quit fooling around with the flashlight. I never considered this a disappointment, though, since neither of us could be called chatty, he by normal country reticence and me in imitation of him and because no one (mothers, grandmothers, and dogs excepted) listened much to the ditherings of small boys.

I believe I was expected to learn about fishing through osmosis. Although I was taught how to hook several kinds of bait and tie a few knots and, eventually, row a boat, I believe any instruction I received was intended to make me less a bother to him and not necessarily a better fisherman. It was not an unkind act, not really, just a practical one.

It was obvious to everyone that I was willing to do anything to be allowed to go fishing. I was not permitted to go alone, however, until my father knew I could swim. So one morning he told me to get my bathing suit and come along. We went to where we kept the rowboat and where there was a small shingle of sandy beach. My father waded in and called for me to come out to him. I did so, quickly and eagerly. He told me to climb on his back and feel how he did it and that when I felt I could do it on my own to slide off and try it alone. I had been fooling around in the brook enough to have lost any fear of the water, and even had a slight idea of a swimming stroke. It was a good thing I did, too, because we swam across the entire lake that morning. We swam and floated and I rested on his back when I was tired. When we started walking home, he told me that

he thought I was a good swimmer but to keep working at it. Then the day was forgotten and neither of us ever mentioned it again.

I was probably eight years old when one morning my father told me we were going to town. He told me to put some good clothes on and wait for him in the Model A. When we got to town, we parked in front of the hardware store. I thought we were there to buy seeds for the garden, the usual supply of nails, wood screws, flashlight batteries, lantern wicks, and, if I was lucky, maybe some popcorn for me.

As usual, once inside I headed for the glass case that held the fishing tackle. Hooks, green and red bobbers with yellow stripes, sinkers, twine, casting line, and a modest assortment of spoons, plugs, spinners, pork rind, and pin-eyed minnows frozen forever in brine were arranged in neat rows on glass shelves. While I gazed into the case, I could hear my father and the clerk discussing a new variety of radish or cucumber off in the distance. Then, while I daydreamed about Pflueger and South Bend reels and True Temper rods, the clerk was suddenly standing next to me and taking a new Akron reel and spool of braided silk casting line from the case. Next he reached up and took down a new steel rod from the rack behind the case. I turned to see who else had come into the store, but discovered that my father and I were still the only customers. My father paid the bill, handed me the bag of seeds, kept the fishing tackle himself, and walked to the car.

All the way home I couldn't speak. I was a bit of a stutterer when I was excited or nervous, and now that I was both, nothing would come out. I knew that the fishing tackle wasn't for me— life wasn't like that. I hadn't earned them. I hadn't done my chores when I should, I had sneaked the dog up to my room, and I had forgotten to oil the lawn mower when I put it away. I couldn't think of anything I'd done right or when it should have been done . . . except feed the chickens and take care of the hounds, my two favorite chores, which I didn't even consider work.

The fishing tackle that my father had bought that day in the hardware store was for me. I had forgotten it was close to my birthday, and never considered that when we went to town it was good sense to buy as much as we could for as far ahead as we could.

My father had found a way to love without showing it or perhaps even admitting it to himself. His way was through our fishing together.

I know now how hard it was for my father to give me those birthday gifts. He was not comfortable when it came to such things as giving presents. He didn't want anyone, especially himself, to know or even think that he might be spoiling me.

I remember that day, though, when I saw him go into the shed where he kept his fishing tackle and come back with the new rod and reel and line. He just handed me the packages and said that he didn't expect to see any weeds in the garden that summer, that he expected to have the lawn mowed without having to remind me a dozen times, and that anything as easily come by could be taken away just as easily. I was almost afraid to accept the gifts. I never wanted them taken away.

It took years for me to understand the complications of a man afraid of love—either giving or receiving it. And it took years for me to realize that among the things I was taught was the same fear—the idea that affection was weak and to be guarded against, and that demonstrating love was fickle and like wishing for something instead of working for it. My father had found a way to love without showing it or perhaps even admitting it to himself. His way was through our fishing together.

When you fish with someone, there's little need for small talk or often any talk at all. There are the small gestures of loving: letting the other cast to a rolling fish, taking the weeds off the other's lure, pointing to a mallard hen with her young, or stopping and listening together while the long call of a loon rolls out across a still cove.

We fished together through the ice of winter and high-running brooks of spring. We fished for spawning perch, bobbed for eels, seined for shiners, waded for hellgrammites, and broomed the grass along spring runs for leopard frogs. For Christmas and holidays, we offered brown parcels that rattled with Jersey Wows, Pikie Minnows, Creek Chub Darters, Hawaiian Wigglers, and Pflueger Chums.

My father grew less harsh, less quick to scold when I was old enough to take the bus to school in town. And when summer came, I often fished with new friends, who would ride their bikes out to our house and spend the night. From that time on, it seems, it was only once in a while that we fished together. I had found a new independence, along with a feeling of escape, and a chance to talk and dream out loud.

I should have seen then that he needed me. Perhaps I did and wouldn't accept it, or perhaps I did but refused to let my well-remembered childhood resentment die. I could be the one who called the dance—yet I didn't. It could wait. "As was the father, so is the the child."

From the army through college, I hardly fished at all. Nor was I really ever home. There was nothing to draw me there that I hadn't learned to live without. The bonds that were never really that tight were easily loosened. Or so I thought until I realized that here I was, now as old as my father had been when we first fished together.

"Want to go fishing?" I asked him when I returned home after being away for many years. "It's the dark of the moon and a long time since we went out and caught a mess of bass."

He didn't have to think about his answer for very long. He just shook his head and said, "No, I don't think so. I've lost interest in it." I smiled and said, "I'll row the boat." But he only shook his head. "Row one of your friends. I gave most of my stuff away."

Hurt and angry, my childhood resentment welling up inside me, I said, "You never gave anybody anything in your life . . . except a whipping." And I went fishing by myself.

On the lake, I felt an uncomfortable sense of satisfaction. I had gotten to him and I knew it. Then I thought, Why? What was the point after all these years? What was the point in being like the part of him I so feared and hated?

I sat in the rowboat where he had sat so many times. I could see myself in my bib overalls, barefooted, sitting at the stern of the boat. I could remember exactly how I felt, how different from him I would be when I grew up. Then I cried into the dark of the moon. I cried aloud, for myself, for my father, for the first time in over twenty years.

I fish because I love to; because I love the environs where trout are found,
which are invariably beautiful . . . and, finally, not because I regard fishing
as being so terribly important but because I suspect that so many
of the other concerns of men are equally important—and not nearly so much fun.

—Robert Traver, *Anatomy of a Fisherman*

From A River Runs Through It by Norman Maclean

After cleaning my fish, I set these three apart with a layer of grass and wild mint.

Then I lifted the heavy basket, shook myself into the shoulder strap until it didn't cut any more, and thought, "I'm through for the day. I'll go down and sit on the bank by my father and talk." Then I added, "If he doesn't feel like talking, I'll just sit."

I could see the sun ahead. The coming burst of light made it look from the shadows that I and a river inside the earth were about to appear on earth. Although I could as yet see only the sunlight and not anything in it, I knew my father was sitting somewhere on the bank. I knew partly because he and I shared many of the same impulses, even to

quitting at about the same time. I was sure without as yet being able to see into what was in front of me that he was sitting somewhere in the sunshine reading the New Testament in Greek. I knew this both from instinct and experience.

Old age had brought him moments of complete peace. Even when we went duck hunting and the roar of the early morning shooting was over, he would sit in the blind wrapped in an old army blanket with his Greek New Testament in one hand and his shotgun in the other. When a stray duck happened by, he would drop the book and raise the gun, and, after the shooting was over, he would raise the book again, occasionally interrupting his reading to thank his dog for retrieving the duck.

The voices of the subterranean river in the shadows were different from the voices of the sunlit river ahead. In the shadows against the cliff the river was deep and engaged in profundities, circling back on itself now and then to say things over to be sure it had understood itself. But the river ahead came out into the sunny world like a chatterbox, doing its best to be friendly. It bowed to one shore and then to the other so nothing would feel neglected.

By now I could see inside the sunshine and had located my father. He was sitting high on the bank. He wore no hat. Inside the sunlight, his faded red hair was once again ablaze and again in glory. He was reading, although evidently only by sentences because he often looked away from the book. He did not close the book until some time after he saw me.

I scrambled up the bank and asked him, "How many did you get?" He said, "I got all I want." I said, "But how many did you get?" He said, "I got four or five." I asked, "Are they any good?" He said, "They are beautiful."

He was about the only man I ever knew who used the word "beautiful" as a natural form of speech, and I guess I picked up the habit from hanging around him when I was little.

"How many did you catch?" he asked. "I also caught all I want," I told him. He omitted asking me just how many that was, but he did ask me, "Are they any good?" "They are beautiful," I told him, and sat down beside him.

"What have you been reading?" I asked. "A book," he said. It was on the ground on the other side of him. So I would not have to bother to look over his knees to see it, he said, "A good book."

Then he told me, "In the part I was reading it says the Word was in the beginning, and that's right. I used to think water was first, but if you

listen carefully you will hear that the words are underneath the water."

"That's because you are a preacher first and then a fisherman," I told him. "If you ask Paul, he will tell you that the words are formed out of water."

"No," my father said, "you are not listening carefully. The water runs over the words. Paul will tell you the same thing. Where is Paul anyway?"

I told him he had gone back to fish the first hole over again. "But he promised to be here soon," I assured him. "He'll be here when he catches his limit," he said. "He'll be here soon," I reassured him, partly because I could already see him in the subterranean shadows.

My father went back to reading and I tried to check what we had said by listening. Paul was fishing fast, picking up one here and there and wasting no time in walking them to shore. When he got directly across from us, he held up a finger on each hand and my father said, "He needs two more for his limit."

I looked to see where the book was left open and knew just enough Greek to recognize λόγος as the Word. I guessed from it and the argument that I was looking at the first verse of John. While I was looking, Father said, "He has one on."

It was hard to believe, because he was fishing in front of us on the other side of the hole that Father had just fished. Father slowly rose, found a good-sized rock and held it behind his back. Paul landed the fish, and waded out again for number twenty and his limit. Just as he was making the first cast, Father threw the rock. He was old enough so that he threw awkwardly and afterward had to rub his shoulder, but the rock landed in the river about where Paul's fly landed and at about the same time, so you can see where my brother learned to throw rocks into his partner's fishing water when he couldn't bear to see his partner catch any more fish.

Paul was startled for only a moment. Then he spotted Father on the bank rubbing his shoulder, and Paul laughed, shook his fist at him, backed to shore and went downstream until he was out of rock range. From there he waded into the water and began to cast again, but now he was far enough away so we couldn't see his line or loops. He was a man with a wand in a river, and whatever happened we had to guess from what the man and the wand and the river did.

As he waded out, his big right arm swung back and forth. Each circle of his arm inflated his chest. Each circle was faster and higher and longer until his arm became defiant and his chest breasted the sky. On shore we were sure, although we could see no line, that the air above him was singing with loops of line that never touched the water but got bigger and bigger each time they passed and sang. And we knew what was in his mind from the lengthening defiance of his arm. He was not going to let his fly touch any water close to shore where the small and middle-sized fish were. We knew from his arm and chest that all parts of him were saying, "No small one for the last one." Everything was going into one big cast for one last big fish.

From our angle high on the bank, my father and I could see where in the distance the wand was going to let the fly first touch water. In the middle of the river was a rock iceberg, just its tip exposed above water and underneath it a rock house. It met all the residential requirements for big fish—powerful water carrying food to the front and back doors, and rest and shade behind them.

My father said, "There has to be a big one out there."

I said, "A little one couldn't live out there."

My father said, "The big one wouldn't let it."

My father could tell by the width of Paul's chest that he was going to let the next loop sail. It couldn't get any wider. "I wanted to fish out there," he said, "but I couldn't cast that far."

Paul's body pivoted as if he were going to drive a golf ball three hundred yards, and his arm went high into the great arc and the tip of his wand bent like a spring, and then everything sprang and sang.

Suddenly, there was an end of action. The man was immobile. There was no bend, no power in the wand. It pointed at ten o'clock and ten o'clock pointed at the rock. For a moment the man looked like a teacher with a pointer illustrating something about a rock to a rock. Only water moved. Somewhere above the top of the rock house a fly was swept in water so powerful only a big fish could be there to see it.

I've Still Got It by Chris Santella

A few years back a non-angling friend called on me for a mission of mercy. His father-in-law, Bill, was coming out to Oregon from Arkansas to visit. Bill was eighty-six, a recent widower, and his health and mobility were none too good. In his youth in Wisconsin, Bill had been quite a trout fisherman. He even contract-tied flies for Orvis. The ostensible purpose of the visit was to see his daughter, but what Bill really wanted was to go fishing. It could be the last time. I set everything up for an afternoon float on the McKenzie, where Bill could fish seated from the boat.

Bill had been characterized as being trenchant, bordering on irascible. Yet none of these unsociable tendencies were in evidence on our ride to Eugene. He recounted fishing memories, listened patiently as I attempted to explain the McKenzie's place in western fishing lore, and near the end of the ride, almost sheepishly, expressed a concern that had been gnawing at him: What if he didn't catch any fish? How would that cap off a life where fishing had played such an important role?

He needn't have worried.

We pushed off from a launch on the lower river, Bill rigged up with a pair of soft hackles. Within five casts, he had his first fish on. By the time we pulled off the river five hours later, he had felt nearly a hundred fish. Many of these went unnoticed, despite our guide's cries of "Set!" Yet still, he brought several dozen fish to hand. That most were scrawny hatchery rainbows mattered not at all. I remember him saying, "I've still got it" at some point in the afternoon.

On the two-hour ride home I drifted in and out of sleep in the backseat while Bill replayed the afternoon to his son-in-law, contrasting the day's exploits with fishing adventures long past.

"I've still got it."

Women Who Fish and the Men Who Love Them by Seth Norman

O let me go down to the stream again,
  To the lonely stream and the sky.
    All I need is a good long rod,
    And a lass who casts a fly.

Freshman year in college and a frat party to which I'd earned an invitation with a tackle that separated several of my favorite bones from their buddies . . . She had red-fox hair, gray eyes and was dressed in the kind of casual clothes I would someday recognize as L.L. Bean. Amidst a beery night of 941 people asking, "So-what's-your-major?" she said, apropos of nothing, "What I'll miss most about home is a very nice smallmouth pond, though in the spring I do have to carry my pistol because of copperheads."

"Marry me," I said.

* * * * *

It can't be pretty, watching me watch a woman fishing. Doesn't much matter if she's twenty-two or seventy-nine, I stand with mouth agape and eyes askew, curious and feeling wild. Keep your *Penthouse* stories of tri-sex on horseback with twins in trains—give me a female of my species staring down a line into dark water. Give me brown neoprene and my imagination supplies black lace. I don't care what kind of angling she's up to. If she's pitched out liver for catfish my barbels start to twitch.

So why aren't there more of them?

This isn't a rhetorical question, and I have no answer save for the obvious: "They're not often trained to do it." We should fix that. Start a campaign with a Madison Avenue game plan: "Warm Water Ms," "NOW About Trout," and "Cosmo Girls Go Nymph." Toss in a column by Abby—"Commit your life to fishing, dear, which will have the side benefit of attracting as many men as anchovies in a school"—then a feature in *Architectural Digest*. "And for her tying room, Angie Perry picked out a plume theme, ostrich and peacock, with accents of Golden Pheasant and carpets suitable for dubbing."

Just ideas. Sincere ideas. Fishing is a sport in which women could and should excel (and sometimes do), from the timing of a precise cast to the fine motor control for tying to #24s. I personally have met women who could land a billfish in one hand and me in the other.

Give Us More, I say. To that end I've spent much of my life trying to encourage social revolution. When young I even earned a reputation for suave lines like "Come on up to my room, I'll show you my Creek Chub" and "If you really want some wahoo, baby, let me tie you up a Bimini Twist."

Yeah, well, some sort of reputation, anyway.

There were the times when I actually did lure damsels to my boat. They almost always had a wonderful time, save for occasional discomfort over bait. One particularly good sport solved this in an ingenious fashion:

"You know," said I, admiringly, "you sure have been good about those squid tentacles. No 'yechh' noises from you, no sir."

Said companion stared at me blankly. "They're plastic," she said.

"Plastic? Ah, no. Not, ah, actually."

At that moment she held the bait knife in one hand and the tentacles in the other. Her eyes had an interesting glint. "Look, pal. We've been having a pretty good time, haven't we? Out in the middle of nature's noplace, where I've swallowed four waves, eaten a soggy, salt sandwich, and broken three nails?"

"Why . . . yes, we sure have!"

"Good. So listen closely while watching these eyes you've admired: these awful things are plastic, aren't they?"

"Absolutely. And so, you know, lifelike, too."

* * * * *

Bait isn't the only discouraging feature for women who've had little experience. Holding fish can cause problems: the thumb-to-forefinger grip so effective with tweezers has limitations when attempted with a thrashing three-pound bass; and though it's probably as good a system as others, choosing a plug because "It's just the most darling little froggie" lacks that scientific flavor I strive for in my own selections. Sometimes even the most basic rules of obsession seem daunting, as happened on one winter steelhead trip.

"Exactly when do we stop?"

"Like I said: when your line keeps freezing in the guides."

"That's the only time?"

"Right."

Wrong, by gosh . . . we *would* stop if I had two hooks of a treble spinner lodged in my hiney. You bet.

* * * * *

Nevertheless, I remain committed to finding or developing female fishing company. I'll admit to keeping evidence of a better-fated trip under my mattress, a "fish-cake" photo in which even the crappie seems to be smiling, probably because in the battle just finished it ended up wearing half the bikini of the lucky angler who holds it. If that image doesn't silence the pervert who whines, "But I fish to get away from women," then set him in this scene.

You wake to the smell of coffee. In she comes, face flushed above her vest. "You," she hums, "were terrific last night."

"Really?"

"My, yes! The way you handled your rod when you laid that drift so naturally along the seam . . ."

"Ah, shucks. But hey, your double-haul to the far bank? And the way you high-sticked that riffle—"

"Stop it! take me—"

"Yes!"

"*Fishing! Now!*"

Young anglers love new rivers the way they love the rest of their lives.
Time doesn't seem to be of the essence
and somewhere in the system is what they are looking for.

—THOMAS McGUANE, "MIDSTREAM," AN OUTSIDE CHANCE

Rainbows Don't Fight Too Good by Tom Boyd

Fly fishing's greatest reward is teaching a youngster to fish. It's wonderful to watch their determination to learn—it sure tickles your funny bone. Kids listen, something we do less of as we grow older. They have little baggage and few bad habits.

My favorite student was Mike "Rip-Their-Lips-Off" Espinoza. Mike was seven, a neat kid with huge blue eyes. He didn't know one end of a fly rod from the other. I showed him the basics of casting then let him have at it. After watching me like in a trance, he took over. It looked like he was floggin' a buggy whip while doing a whacked-out Zorro impersonation. "Slow down a bit, Mike," I said.

Slow down he did—as in slow motion. The rod took about an hour to hit behind him, the line a soggy noodle.

"Is that the way I cast, Mike?"

"Exactly," he replied. I cringed.

The Conejos River in Colorado has huge rainbows. Unfortunately, it had just been stocked with puny imitations. I tied an egg pattern on, then dodged Mike's rod as he somehow managed almost respectable casts. Naturally, he also drilled every form of vegetation in the area. The grim reaper couldn't have done it better. The trees thirty feet behind us were safe so far. Mike had miraculously missed them. Then WHAM! A strike! Mike set the hook! I mean SET the hook! This fifty-pound boy ripped that puny little rainbow out of the water like it was shot from a cannon. Plop! It landed in a tree.

Mike looked at the tree, startled, eyes wide. "Ah, he just came right out!"

"You bet, Mike, like he was launched. You ripped his lips off."

"Maybe he could jump that far?" Mike asked sheepishly.

Mike, on my shoulders, retrieved the dangling fish.

"Any lips left, Mike?" Mike, giggling, ran the little bugger over to the river and plopped him in.

"I bet he liked the hatchery a lot better'n this," said Mike.

Mike caught another pathetic fish. "Rainbows don't fight too good," Mike declared.

"Well, not these guys. Wanna try for some wild ones?"

Trujillo Meadows held good rainbows. Mike buggy-whipped his woolly bugger out to thirty-five feet, where a five-pound rainbow hit it like a cop after a doughnut, almost wrenching the rod from Mike's hand. The kid was in shock, but held firm on the rod. Hollering at a fever pitch, he was dragged down the beach into the water. Running in after him, I picked him up wriggling and hollering—but still reeling—and flung him onto the bank. Again he was dragged down the beach. I was yelling instructions, but Mike wasn't listening much.

"Who's got who, Mike?"

"He's getting away! Help!"

"Nah. Rainbows don't fight too good, Mike."

What a sight! Mike drenched; me drenched; Mike hollering; me laughing, watching this determined youngster battling his first real fish on a fly rod. And what a fish—a rocket ship acting like someone had just slipped him a habanero pepper. The epic struggle lasted twenty minutes until Mike got the big bow close to shore. With a last burst of energy, the rainbow leaped high, right at our feet. The tippet broke, but somehow the fish landed in the middle of my outstretched net.

Mike kept shouting, "Holy cow! Wow! Holy cow!" as we lay in the water, drenched, dirty, laughing hysterically. I'll bet no one ever again heard Mike say, "Rainbows don't fight too good."

So that's my tale—believe it or not.

*Fishing consists of a series of misadventures
interspersed by occasional moments of glory.*

—Howard Marshall, Reflections in a River

Tokay, Trout, and Trouble by Mark Cloutier

It kind of slipped out over dinner: I knew as I was saying it that I should have stopped or changed the subject, but it was too late. At best, all I could do was make my proposal sound fairly unattractive. It was to be the good lady wife's last day of her holidays so I suggested I take a day off work and partake in a kind of picnic day out in the fresh air, maybe by a picturesque trout stream, maybe I could take the fly rod!

"Can I bring the dog?" was her inquiry. I said yes before I could stop myself: as I say, it kind of slipped out. And from that point on I felt that this day would be like no other—it was possibly the last chance for me to fish before

season's end and I felt somewhat puzzled at the predicament I had got myself into. Surely the last Friday in May was a time to fish for the last rising trout of the season, to reflect on the angling days past and plan for angling days future.

"We'll have to be up before six a.m. and out the door to beat peak hour traffic." I thought that this would give me an opening, a way out of silly fishing and back into the serious stuff.

"OK," was Sharon's response.

The four-day forecast was to be for a perfect day. It was on, I was locked in and had to make the most of it.

At the old white bridge over the river I went

through the peculiar fly-fishing ritual of donning all the necessary paraphernalia; I certainly looked the part, but as the dog raced past me and into the river and then proceeded through the first pool, I guess you could say my heart wasn't in it.

Before I go on I should give you a brief picture of Tokay, a twelve-month-old golden retriever pup. "Pup" is probably inaccurate in terms of size, for at nearly forty kilos he is as strong and as big a dog as you could wish for. "Pup" is definitely the correct way to describe his state of mind, though, as everything is a game or adventure. A trout stream was bliss for this big, loafing, floppy yellow dog.

To say that he has a love of water is totally inaccurate. I would call it a single-minded infatuation: if there is water within a hundred yards, then he will be in it. It is impossible to keep him from rivers, lakes, ponds, pools, or puddles— surely not the greatest of fishing companions. Ah, but at least Sharon would keep him under control; he was already in the RED class at obedience training, whatever that meant.

So the first pool was ruined by him swimming through it. I could live with that—I never get a fish from the first pool anyway. It was the next deep run where some good fish lay. I fished a deep rubber-legged nymph that was more of a lure than a nymph. The indicator dipped, but I missed the fish. I cursed as I felt sure that a little luck would be needed to get a fish this day. I glanced at the bank and saw Sharon, but could not see the dog. I looked behind to see him with a mouth full of fly line that I had let trail downstream.

"No! No!" I screamed as Tokay chomped his way up the line like some real-life Pac Man. I quickly pulled the line in, but a coil was still hooked around one of his teeth. I tried to pull it free but it was still hooked and he pulled back. As the line seesawed through his great white teeth, it occurred to me that I was actually giving him a dental floss with an eighty-dollar imported fly line!

Sharon lay on the bank in the glorious sun, the lead in her hand and the dog moving through the next run and pool. I bypassed the dog, and Sharon (after mentioning something about dog obedience being a waste), in the vain hope of finding a piece of undisturbed water. I did find a quiet bend, where lo and behold I actually caught a small scrappy trout. Guess who rounded the bend and, on seeing the trout splashing across the surface, fairly charged at the poor fish?

The dog was in the water almost instantly, snapping only inches behind the defenseless fish. In one movement I accelerated the fish by dragging it along the surface and swinging it through the air, the plan being for me to grasp it, unhook it, and release it unharmed. The fish did swing toward me, but I missed it, and as it swung back like a pendulum it disappeared into Tokay's jaws with a crocodile-like chomp! I prised the dog's teeth apart, extracted the trout, which was miraculously still alive, and released it.

The day did not change much. I missed two rising trout at the tail-out of a pool because the dog became tangled in the trailing fly line (yet again). Sharon was still on the bank, still with the lead in her hand.

I kind of lost the plot after that, and on seeing Tokay eat the crusty top of a cow pad and proceed to roll in the moist center, I wondered about the two-hour trip home. Believe it or not, Sharon tried to assure me that if she had not been there to control the dog (remember he is in RED class), then things would have been far worse!

A Story by Bob White

I've always had a soft spot for older guys. It started when I was five or six years old and my family lived in a part of town that not too many years before had been farmland. Many of the old farmhouses, though often in need of repair, still stood in stark contrast to the newer homes around them. Across the street from where I lived was a field overrun with wild flowers, blackberries, and wild roses. I remember the old house that stood in it to be low slung, in need of paint, and with a porch like the Radley house, in Harper Lee's *To Kill a Mockingbird*. The old widower who lived there kept mostly to himself and was rarely seen. Of course, this made for all sorts of childhood speculation, particularly around Halloween.

I don't recall his name, but I do remember that he trapped the woods and creed bottom where I played. He always tended his traps early in the morning, long before I returned from kindergarten, but occasionally I'd see him skinning a raccoon or a fox in his back yard. Once in a while he'd nod as I passed and eventually we became friends. He never said much, but he taught me how to keep a knife sharp, skin an animal, and light a kitchen match with my thumbnail. I always enjoyed our time together, and felt a loss when he died. After-

wards, the brambles around the old place seemed to take over, and the house had all but disappeared in honeysuckle by the time we moved a few years later.

We moved to a neighborhood that was a kid's dream. On the edge of the country, we had woods to play in, fields to fly kites, creeks to catch crawdads, and lakes to fish. At the end of our street lived an old fellow who held all of us in awe. Mister Wittenbrink, rumor had it, had been in World War I, had suffered shell shock, and was deaf. He lived alone, and without the ability to hear, or anyone to speak with, his speech had degraded to the point where he could barely talk. He was a master fisherman, however, and when he was preparing for a day at the lake, he had no trouble communicating his glee with us kids. The ritual began with him walking thoughtfully around in his garden. When he determined that the place was right, he'd thrust his pitchfork into the ground and start strumming it. Within a few minutes worms would be writhing on the ground for yards around. He'd grunt and giggle at the bounty of the bait at his feet. When he was sufficiently armed with plump night-crawlers, he'd pile all of his gear into an old wheelbarrow and set off for the lakes,

making a low humming noise. In the evening he'd return with a wheelbarrow full of carp and the occasional catfish. We'd all gather around to watch him clean his catch while he laughed and made a particular clicking noise that I still associate with a wheelbarrow full of carp.

One day there were a number of cars at the Wittenbrink place. He had died and his family had come to clean the house and put it up for sale. It never occurred to me that he had a family, and I remember wondering why they'd never gone fishing with him. He was a happy man—I never saw him otherwise, even with all of the troubles he must have seen.

My Grandpa White cinched my affection for older guys. John was a man who seemed to remember the value of children, and was always a true friend to them. Once, at a formal Easter brunch, I knocked over a glass of orange juice. My father dropped his head—my mother looked alarmed— Grandma was already coming up out of her chair. I looked painfully at John, who winked and bumped over his glass of wine.

"Oh my," he gasped. "That'll probably stain. Bob, why don't you go to the kitchen for some water. Mother, should we put baking soda on it?"

When I was ten or eleven, I started hanging around the high-school ball fields to watch the older guys at their practice.

"Do you #@%&-ing believe it?" one of the players would say.

"#@%&-ing right!" another answered.

It seemed to me that every other word they used was a variation of the word "#@%&."

That night at dinner, I looked across the table at one of my sisters and politely asked, "Phyllis, would you please pass the #@%&-ing potatoes?"

My father, unaccustomed to ten-year-old boys with such table manners, had me by the shirt and in the next room before my mother had taken her second gasp.

"What'd I say . . . what'd I say?" I squealed. "I don't know what it means!"

My father, sensing the truth when he heard it, lowered me to the floor and mumbled, "You'll have to talk to your mother."

The next day my mother read me a wonderful story about flowers, pollen, stamens, and all sorts of interesting things. When she finished she closed the book and looked at me expectantly. "Mom, what does #@%& mean?" I asked.

"Go on out and play," she instructed. "And don't say that word again."

That night Grandpa White called the house and asked for me. "You busy tomorrow?" he asked. "I've got some work around the place that I need your help with."

As I recall, my mother dropped me off on her way to the grocery store, and we got right to work. John was ripping a bunch of wood on his table saw, and my job was to hold the boards as they came off of the saw and stack them by size in the corner. After we were covered in sawdust and the shop smelled of pine, he announced a break. We sat on his bench and sipped a special concoction of his, a mixture of 7UP and grape juice. "I hear you got in Dutch with your father last night," he began.

"Something I said at supper . . . Mom read me a book about flowers yesterday."

"So . . . what'd you say?"

"#@%&," I replied. "Grandpa . . . what's it mean?"

"Well . . . you'll figure out the plumbing part of it all by yourself," he said, and then went on to tell me about love, respect, and

commitment. It wasn't until I was much older that I understood just how special Grandpa White was.

Years later, I found myself in Alaska, working at a fly-out fishing lodge as a guide. First-year guides are at the bottom of the food chain, and always expected the worst when the Boss announced the next day's fishing assignments. New guides are rarely asked whom they might want to fish with—in fact, few guests are even asked that question. The operator of any fishing lodge is constantly walking a tightrope in an effort to keep everyone happy, and asking such questions is a path that is best not traveled.

After I'd been around a few years and began to play a small part of planning the next day's schedule, I have to admit that I'd arrange to fish with certain guests when I could. I rarely let an older guy leave the lodge without making the opportunity to spend time on the water with him.

It was the end of September, and the end of another season. Although no one knew it yet, it marked the end of my tenure as a fishing guide in Alaska. I'd arranged to spend my last day on the Agulawok River with a woman and her older father. She'd fished at the lodge several times over the past years with her friends, but I'd never met her father, Bill, who was a quiet and distinguished gentleman. He was a bit unsure on his feet, and although I know it killed him to do so, he fished while sitting most of the time. Sunny, his daughter, let me know that her father was dying.

"We're all dying . . . ." I said, a bit uncomfortable with the knowledge.

"This will probably be our last trip," she continued. "This is how we want to remember our last days together."

It was a difficult time for me personally. I knew that I'd be leaving Alaska in just a few days, and walking away from the life that I loved. Over the past month, I'd found myself saying goodbye to a different river every day, knowing that even if I did return one day, it would be different. I wouldn't be the guy on the oars, or in the water, walking the boat. But, for all my troubles, and as hard as it was for me, it must have been incredibly difficult for Bill and his daughter. "Then, let's make it a day to remember." It was all I could think of to say.

It was a perfect autumn day, and the late morning fog softened the dark shadows that fell across the water as we ran upriver to start our first drift. The breeze chilled our noses and the sun warmed our hair. Bill sat with his back to the wind and I watched as he gracefully took it all in.

Few words were shared in the boat that morning—few were really necessary. We were all quietly and desperately trying to hold on to the moment for our very different but similar reasons. Sometime before lunch, Bill struck a deep and powerful Arctic Char. This was a fish that necessitated pulling the boat to shore and beaching—and not just for show. Few fish are as beautiful as a September Char, and as Bill held it in the water to revive it, he asked me to take its photograph.

"Don't you want to be in it?" I asked.
"Nah, just the fish . . . would you look at him!"

"Is he ready to go?" I asked, as I finished taking the shot.

"One last look," Bill replied. "Just . . . one last look."

That day ran its course as they all seem to, and it was time to drift down to the bottom of the river and return to the lodge. The whole way downriver I watched as Bill gazed out over the valley—looking one last time.

. . . the most honest, ingenious, harmless art of Angling.

—Izaak Walton, *The Compleat Angler*

Confessions of an Eco-Redneck by Steve Chapple

Each cast I made, inept or elegant, resulted in a hookup. . . . Though no innocent, I was in such a state of giddy hysteria I soon forgot to pay much attention to my back cast.

I heard a scream. I turned around. I had hooked my four-year-old son in the cheek. That is, the hook had entered his mouth and got stuck on the inside. He was a brave little boy. He didn't cry, probably from the shock of it. There was a trickle of blood. His mother dropped her fly rod and rushed over.

We drove quickly to the emergency room. The irony of a father hooking his son during the Mother's Day caddis hatch was not lost on me (or on my wife). The Park Street Clinic in Livingston (Montana) is located on the river, beside the 9th Street Bridge. Thousands of caddis flies batted against the windows as we waited. The doctor introduced himself. He popped open my son Jack's cheek with a gloved finger, gingerly.

"Number 14 Parachute Adams," the doctor pronounced. "Am I right?"

We had come to the right place. With a hank of what looked like dental floss, the doctor lassoed the Parachute Adams, a caddis imitation, and extracted its pinched barb without a whimper from Jack, though his mother was about ready to faint. For my part, I was relieved. There was still a good hour of fishing time before sunset.

A trout is vulnerable to the fisherman
because he eats.

—Vincent. C. Marinaro, *In the Ring of the Rise*

The Shore Supper by Jon Wurtmann

Spadone and I grew up together. Like any life-long friends, we know each other too well. Our humor is coded, proprietary, and deeply cutting. Parents ourselves, we still rebel against ours. We have our own language, customs, and floating rituals. There is the unwinding Chip Schechter story, a bizarre tale of a boy, his dysfunctional family, and his pet chipmunk, Skippy. It's a story that we've told for years now, each year picking up where we left off. We'll float for miles—in character—playing out various impromptu scenarios. Heard from the bank, it must surely be a strange and curious thing.

There is the ritual of gear lending. Pete is historically undergunned in the rod department, and I've lent him rods and reels over the years to the point where I finally ended up

buying him one. And then of course, there is the shore supper.

All year long we threaten to take another fishing trip. Most years we actually manage to. It's always a mellow, trouty river: the Connecticut, the Delaware. Recently, we've broken out and done the Florida Keys and Baja. But the river trips remain most fondly in my memory.

We plan the trip around the peak hatches and long days of early summer. We establish a base camp: a tent, lean-to, or a cheap hotel. This allows us to run day trips down different stretches every day. If the action is hot, we'll gladly repeat a stretch. Problem is, the best fishing is always at dusk, and it's a long day without dinner. Hence, the shore supper.

Over morning coffee, we load the canoe with

the old Coleman two-burner stove, cooler, and mess kit. In the cooler is pre-cut chicken, onions, garlic, carrots, broccoli, tomatoes, ginger, cilantro, various spices, and our mutual weakness, basmati rice.

As a teenager, Spadone traveled to India, Afghanistan, and Morocco. He came back twenty pounds lighter from the dysentery, and infected with an undying love of curry. We drove his folks nuts re-creating authentic Indian curries in their hermetic suburban kitchen; grinding spices, making homemade cheese, and introducing strange new smells to the household. Now, we make our curries on the stream.

Around six in the evening, after a long day of fishing, we begin to scout the location. The sun is still high, and there's no point in flogging the water. Might as well eat. We look for a grassy bank, a big flat rock. We know the place by its karma.

One of us sets up the stove, pumps it, and lights the fragrant blue flames. The other cracks the first beers of the day, and acts as sous-chef. First the rice is peppered with bay leaves, cardamom seeds, cumin, coriander, cloves, and saffron and set on a low flame. In the main skillet the chicken pieces are quickly seared, removed, and set aside. Next into the hot skillet, ginger, onion, and garlic begin to sizzle. The first wafts of dinner start to drift over the water.

Once the onion is translucent, the spices follow. Red or green curry, perhaps some Thai fish sauce if we remembered to bring it. Then the tomatoes, carrots, and broccoli are thrown into the sputtering mix. Downwind, a murmuring begins among the diligent anglers, casting furiously, trying to eke out the most from their day astream.

Coconut milk is next. Oh sweet mercy, coconut milk: heaven in a can. Now the curry is creamy, rich, brown, and simmering. We add the chicken

pieces and the cilantro and set the skillet on low to allow everything to marry and thicken. Perhaps there's a fresh beer.

Soon, it's suppertime. No plates—just the two skillets—we dish equal amounts of rice and curry into the other and begin. By now, the sweet foreign smell of exotic spices has formed a cloud above the river, intoxicating the hatching insects and causing the passing drifters to crane their necks. It smells like Delhi on the Delaware.

In the slanting light of the late afternoon, we linger and savor the meal. Relive the small glories of today's fish, and prepare ourselves for the evening rise. Coffinflies? Shadflies? Brown Drake Spinners? Our anticipation rises as we fold the stove, throw the plates in the cooler, and shove off into the evening current.

Recipes feed two hungry river rats. To save time on stream, dice, chop, and bag all ingredients in advance. You can also combine spices and the rice in advance.

Catskill Coffinfly Curry

Oil for cooking
1   large onion diced
6   fat cloves garlic diced
1   large chunk fresh ginger diced
3   carrots sliced
2   tomatoes sliced
1   cup broccoli sliced (you can use the stems also)
    Curry powder or paste (Thai Kitchen makes
        excellent paste curries)
    Thai fish sauce to taste
    One can coconut milk (available in low-cal
        or full strength)
2   boneless chicken breasts cubed
    Cilantro to taste

See above for cooking. Serve over rice with chutney and with cucumber salad on the side.

Baetis Basmati Rice

1   cup Basmati rice
1²/₃ cup water
     Large pinch saffron fronds
1   tsp. cardamom seeds
1   tsp. coriander seeds
1   tsp. cumin seeds
10   cloves
4   bay leaves

Combine everything, bring to boil, cover, and reduce heat. Simmer for 15–20 minutes until water is absorbed. Stir and remove from heat.

Caddis Cucumber Salad

1   large ripe tomato, sliced
1   shallot, sliced thin
2   Tbsp. fresh dill minced
    Oil and lemon juice to taste
    Salt and pepper to taste
1   cucumber

Combine tomato, shallot, dill, lemon juice, oil, salt, and pepper in a Tupperware bowl up to 24 hours in advance. Keep refrigerated. Do not add the cucumber, as it will bruise and discolor. Just before serving, peel and slice the cucumber into the salad mixture, toss, and serve. A very refreshing antidote to the curry!

The Creek by Scott Slater

There's a creek, a special creek, that has a place in my heart. This creek holds the memory of my first trout on the fly.

One beautiful summer's evening my father and I were driving back from one of our many unsuccessful, exploratory trout-fishing expeditions. As we crossed a bridge over the upper reaches of the stream that we had just spent a good part of the day trying to get to, a trout broke the surface in the small reed-infested pool below. We pulled the car over a few yards up the road and I took out my fly rod while Dad went for the more familiar spinning tackle.

A closer examination of the roadside pool revealed three fish feeding. Dad stood back while I struggled to cast a reasonable distance. Perhaps more by sheer luck than by skill, the line straightened and the fly landed ten yards down the pool. I twitched my hand-tied Cock-y-bondhu (tied using cotton, a size 1 2 mullet hook and a hackle torn from a squid jig) across the now active pool. Halfway through the retrieve, a small boil within the vicinity of my fly indicated that the rod should be lifted. Although I struck much too fast, the hook still went home.

I played the fish out, in a way that would have been expected of a self-taught, eigh-year-old fly fisher (the trout was in complete control). The fish tired. I began to bring it toward the bridge but my progress was halted by a wall of reeds. Fortunately, my father stepped into the water and grasped my fish by the tail. When he presented me with my

prize, a beautiful brown hen of half a pound, I let out a cry of joy for all the world to hear.

That was six years ago. The pool that gave me my first trout is now a carpet of reeds. I think back to that evening and wonder what my life would have been if I had not spied that rise? I ask myself what would have happened if we had driven over that bridge only to see a still pool of water? If that had been the case, then I doubt I would have returned. This is a terrifying thought, for without the place I call "the creek," my life would simply not be complete, and I think I'll tell you why.

This creek is no more than a yard across in most places, but it contains a good head of trout. Most of the fish in this water are not much larger than 300 grams; however, there are larger ones of up to eight pounds in some of the better pools.

In this creek, just putting the fly on the water is far more important than a lifelike presentation. These trout are rarely fussy and in six years of fishing the creek I have only had seven or eight refusals.

Casting room is sparse with most back casts ending up in a tree. Bow-and-arrow and roll casts are usually the only appropriate casting methods. In a lot of cases, a method that we like to call "the dangle treatment" accounts for almost half of the fish we put on the grass.

It took me quite a while to realize just how many trout inhabit the insignificant parts of this stream. I think a lot of fly fishers would get a bit of a surprise if they walked up to a stretch of water little more than a foot across and six inches deep, only to see a small bow-wave as a little brownie darts away.

I have named many of the smarter trout—there's Albert, Humphrey, Rocky, and Ray, to name a few. Of all the hundreds of trout I have presented a fly to, Albert is my favorite. Over the years I have watched him grow from an eight-inch fingerling to a plump thirteen incher of a bit more than a pound. After six years he still cruises in the same pattern, even though he has put on a considerable amount of weight. He circles a clump of reeds, then he heads into the shallows, then around a dead tree and back to the clump of reeds again.

Have I ever caught him, you ask? Ah, well, I have once, and I've pricked him on several occasions. As hard as it may be to believe, I see

These days I don't keep any of the trout I catch. I have developed far too much respect for the fish in this creek to ever kill one.

Albert as more of a friend than an enemy, although I doubt he feels the same about me.

These days I don't keep any of the trout I catch. I have developed far too much respect for the fish in this creek to ever kill one.

My father often says to me that one day I will find another special fishery, be it a river, lake, or stream, but I've fished in some magnificent and beautiful places that go by the names of Tumut, Murrumbidgee, Eucumbene, and Toolondo, none of which are as special to me as the creek.

The creek has given me so many fond memories of my father and my childhood, as well as some great fishing. The creek presented me with my first trout and I hope that it shall spare me my last. . . .

Lifelines by Gary Ferguson

We were hardly prodigies, my brother and me. Just lucky. By ten years old we had a firm grip on the good life, having been introduced by a hiccup of a creek barely six feet wide and eight inches deep, so small it didn't even have a name, a creek pouring from the knots of a hedgerow into a perfect slice of hardwood, then losing itself barely a half-mile later, in a boat channel full of catfish and weeds. Soon after our first wallow we started hustling jobs mowing and raking lawns for the forty bucks we needed to buy two pairs of green rubber boots, which we used to walk the bottoms of that stream week after week, spring to fall—past the pawpaw and pussy willow, past jewelweed and violets and horsetail. Into dark, secret places. Places we were sure no kid had ever gone.

The way I figure, it was those dances with a no-name creek that, years later, led to my work as a naturalist, living on the east bank of Idaho's Salmon River in a sagging, one-room cabin with no indoor plumbing. Cooking my pasta and brewing coffee in what days before had been snow in the Sawtooths; bathing by way of a cold swim in the river, which in late summer meant going elbow to fin with hundreds of Chinook salmon, red and ragged from nearly a thousand miles swimming upstream from the Pacific to lay eggs in the same sprawls of gravel they'd hatched in years before. At my campfire programs, people were always asking what those salmon did when they came to a fork. How could they possibly know which way to go?

"They can taste the home stream," I'd tell them, as amazed as they were. "A few parts per million—that's all it takes."

Sometimes on my days off I'd hike along the headwaters, bend over and fill my Sierra Cup and drink real slow, imagining that I too could taste home in that water.

Now, at forty-five, I've come to what may well be my last best flow. Another creek, this one fresh out of Montana's Beartooth Mountains, fast-stepping past my back door on its way to the plains. These days I take my walks along the bottoms with a fly rod in hand, though something tells me when I'm an old man I'll think it just fine to go out there and sit on a slab of granite in a curtain of spray and talk to the willow and herons, the dippers and ducks, forgetting all about the need to fish. A part of me kind of hopes my brother will be likewise unhinged—that some autumn day I'll look out the window and see him tottering up the walk, in his arms a pair of green rubber boots.

It was no big surprise for me to discover that the myths and religions of cultures around the world are so thoroughly washed in the urge to weep and sing, baptize and bury according to the river. Far more confounding is that we could ever forget such kinship, that we could silt or poison the last bright waters without crumpling to our knees, that a man could turn his back on the river without breaking his heart for good.

Sisterly Love by Bevin Wallace

Fly fishing was supposed to be different from other sports, different from the competitive, uncivilized ones where people kept score. Fly fishing was for the meditative, self-actualized set. Right.

I'd always had this image of quietly wading through glassy water, making beautiful arcing casts while lost in thought. Maybe I'd catch a fish but it was almost an afterthought. I hadn't pictured a gang of sunburned brothers, wives, girlfriends, cousins, even parents comparing fish stories, the volume increasing with the gin consumption. But that was the nightly scene at my husband's family's fishing lodge on the Madison.

The worst part was that it always seemed to be just the women in the running for "top rod," which was surely the result of some misdirected sense of chivalry among the men. Although I was new to the family, most everybody knew that I spent a good deal of my time untangling my Adams from the willows. Each time a brother would bring a new tanned and tomboyish girl up to Montana, instead of making a new friend, I had another rival. All my insecurities—about everything from my lousy casting to my mousey hair—would get wrapped up in my inability to catch a big fish.

I told myself I didn't care; it was stupid and missed the whole point of fly fishing. When one of these girls inevitably landed a twenty-three-inch brown on her first day out, I would smile as I watched her bask in the glow of attention and "you're a natural" praise. I'd smugly think, "Good for her; poor girl won't be here again next summer anyway."

I started losing interest in fly fishing. I agreed to float one day several Augusts ago mostly because I didn't want to be a booking weirdo who passes up a paid-for float trip on the Madison. It was hot, the river almost steamy. No one was catching anything except the occasional whitefish. There was absolutely no wind, and after I insisted on losing the elaborate hopper-nymph setup my husband had tied on for me, I started casting like I'd imagined I could. I knew I would catch a fish. So when a well-fed rainbow belted my Royal Wulff, I wasn't startled, and I hooked him almost with a natural reflex. The family watching from the other boats started cheering as I fought the fish, and when we pulled the boat over to land him, my brother-in-law drunkenly jumped ship and splashed over to see my fish. My husband insisted on taking a picture, and I gripped and grinned, basking in the glow with real, almost embarrassing joy.

The rainbow swam away and I hope never gave me another thought. I wish I could say I didn't like being top rod—that I was above caring—but I can't. The next time a young cutie caught the day's big fish, I smiled with genuine happiness for her and didn't even bother to mention that she'd caught it on a wooly bugger drug along the bottom.

Hangover on the Swing by Chris Santella

My first fly-fishing buddy had an after-school job as a stock clerk at a local grocery chain in suburban Connecticut. This was very propitious, as he was in a position to spirit intact beers from wounded six packs, jugs of red wine with maimed labels and other sundry items to the back dumpster . . . a section of the back dumpster where they could be recovered for use at a later date. There were no microbrews or fine Napa Cabernets among the discarded beverages, but as we were under legal drinking age and vastly underfunded, we did not complain.

Before our first big fishing trip—a long weekend in June up to Grand Lake Stream in Maine—my friend secured good stocks of half-skunked Schlitz, Old Milwaukee, and Paul Masson Burgundy, all courtesy of Stop & Shop. He also picked up a plastic bag of generic cigars—about twenty for $3—as we'd heard that cigar smoke would discourage the black flies.

We made it up to Grand Lake Stream in Pete's sputtering Datsun pick-up, set up camp, and against the odds managed to land a few land-locked salmon on Grey Ghost streamers. On our second night we were in an especially celebratory mood, and moved from the Schlitz to the jug wine, augmenting each toast with puffs from our cigars. Not knowing any better, I inhaled the smoke of these no-name cigars, helping to insure the worst hangover of my young life.

When I arose in darkness the next morning and struggled into my waders, it took several minutes for me to realize just how sick I felt. Yet it was our last day on Grand Lake Stream, and I'd be damned if I wasn't going to fish. I staggered into the water, and after a few casts, a nice landlocked took my streamer as it swung in the current. I ratcheted that fish in, knocked it on the head to take home to my parents, and crawled back in the tent in a vain effort to sleep the previous evening away.

The World's Greatest Trout Stream by Russell Chatham

Some of you may be wondering how it is I have the brass to follow the title of this story with the story itself. Everything I tell you will be the absolute truth. Hard as you may search, however, you will find no clues as to the locale of this extraordinary water. The reason, which is simple enough, is that this may be the only place left on Earth to be so pristine and untouched. . . . You can't fly in, because of the forest and rough terrain. A hard day's walk takes you to the start of the fishing, which lies at the head of a violent two-mile series of holes, rapids, and waterfalls.

I saw the first pool in deep shadow early one morning from a vantage point somewhat elevated and back from the river. It was just starting to become autumn. I stared at it while standing by the fire with my friends Larry, Moe, and Curly. At the time, I didn't know we were seeing the world's greatest trout stream.

Larry, the titular head of our do-it-yourself crowd, was the first to point out the trout. They weren't that hard to see, really; it's just that they were so big you could easily mistake them for rocks or sticks or moss. There were two: the small one would be six or seven pounds, the larger one a couple of pounds heavier.

This piece of visual information took a few moments to process. I felt the way you do when you come down the outside of a fast Ferris wheel. I rubbed my eyes idiotically, like one of the dwarfs in Snow White. Then the lenses focused, and I was burning a hole in the water, watching the slow deliberations of these enormous trout.

Sometimes they lay motionless in the crystal-clear water, which was as emerald green as a crown jewel in the early-morning light. Then they would describe a long oval, perhaps defining their territory, or searching for a bit of food. Their world was perhaps a hundred feet long, fifty wide, and eight deep at its deepest point, which is not a very large area to support two creatures such as these. Perhaps there were others, too, up in the fast water where we couldn't see them.

Taking charge, Larry directed Moe to be the first angler. I was envious, but oddly relieved, because I didn't have to worry about blowing what was clearly going to be one bitch of a cast. Luckily, Moe was pretty handy with a fly rod.

Moving into position fifty feet behind the lower fish, the larger one, Moe whipped out a beauty, placing his dry fly half a dozen feet beyond the trout.

On the flat, slow surface, his fly looked like a perky little sailboat. It sailed over the fish evidently unnoticed.

Larry, who was watching along with us from a respectable distance, called out to advise Moe that he might have to change to a nymph. Moe agreed.

The weighted nymph made the cast harder, but Moe punched it out there and the ugly stonefly landed with a plop. The big rainbow nailed it with the speed and violence of a bitchy actress slapping a busboy who tries to reach for her tinkler.

Terrorized, Moe struck, the fly pulled out, and the fish sped to a hiding place. Moe was furious.

"Never mind," called Larry. "Move up and cast to the other one."

This time the fly had time to sink a little, before the second trout took with a force equal to that of its poolmate. And in spite of Moe's every caution, the fly didn't stick this time, either.

After a stern debate over hook styles, timing, and the fish's heritage, we started upstream. Our route took us some distance above the stream, through many different kinds of cactus and sinewy hanging vines, which could entrap and strangle you to death if you weren't careful. The others were far ahead of me. For purposes of this tale, think of me as Oliver Hardy.

Within a fairly brutal half hour, I caught up with the boys, who were peering over a boulder about the size of an elephant.

"You're up, Ollie," said Moe. "Where the hell you been?"

"My feet were writing a check my heart had trouble cashing."

Below the rock I could see the fish. Larry said it was a six-pounder. From down on the stream,

I could no longer see beneath the water because of the glare, so Larry yelled directions.

I had a handsome little caddis fly tied on, but this fish refused to rise to it, so I replaced it with a Trueblood Otter nymph. I heard the yells before feeling the fish.

My line slackened, and I realized the fish was coming downstream toward me. I hand-stripped line, and the fish glided past, every detail sharp through the aquiline water. I noticed in particular the huge square tail. The trout easily took a hundred feet of line before the hook pulled out. We had another discussion.

There was no discernible trail along the river, and again Larry led us up into the thorns. When I caught up this time, the boys were looking down a hundred feet or so into a cauldron of white-and-light-green foamy water. Back where it cleared and darkened, two trout were lying deep down near the bottom. The small one was perhaps a five-pounder, the other at least a couple of pounds more. It was Curly's turn to fish, and we knew he was going to have some trouble with this for several reasons. First of all, he was pretty new at fly fishing. Second, there was only one place to stand to fish the hole, and he would have no visibility. Third, the noise of the nearby falls was approximately like that of a jet taking off, so he would not be able to hear any directions. Larry briefed him and sent him in with a pat on the butt.

It was a painful display. After countless false casts, he managed to lob one up ahead of the fish. One of them seized his fly, but because of the slack line being pushed at him by the current, he couldn't see or feel the take. And because of the thundering falls, he couldn't hear us screaming ourselves hoarse.

With all diligence, he kept flinging his fly back

into the pool. We could see the angst on his face even from far away. Presently, the other fish struck and spit out the fly, just as the first had done.

We gestured to Curly to come up, so we could explain what had happened. He looked like a cross between a man who had sat on a whoopee cushion and someone whose wife had just confessed her infidelities with an entire sports team.

We walked on and soon arrived at a clearing that was truly a part of the dream I had had three and a half decades earlier. The valley opened up to let in more sunlight. The air was now a sublime seventy-five degrees, and the water so clear at times that you were almost convinced there wasn't any. The pool was relatively shallow, with a riffle coming into it on a slow gradient. We could see there were at least four fish in the pool, all more than four pounds.

Larry, as mentor and counsel, was refusing to take the rod, so once again it was Moe's turn to be the entertainment.

Two of the fish were holding high in the water toward the tail of the pool. Moe waded to within forty feet of them and laid out an excellent cast. One of the fish took with a slow, deliberate turn to the side. Moe struck, and we all simultaneously cheered as the trout ran forward into the hole at great speed. The hook pulled out, and Moe's rod stood lifeless.

A certain purplish tone invaded his face, and subsequently his speech, as he came ashore. We didn't say much. After all, how much more was there to say about hook design?

We decided to sit back from the pool and have a little lunch. The soft tundra made a good picnic spot. As we munched and chatted, we could see four or five trout huddled deep in the center of the hole, just below a big rock that deflected the current.

Half an hour later, Larry said to me, "I believe it's your cast, Ollie. Throw a few flies at this spooked group, just in case one of them is feeling better."

I drilled many fine casts here and there, but nothing moved. I think those trout were digging some sort of hole with their fins, in order to have a better place to hide.

"Let's get along," said Larry. "If I'm not mistaken, there are mucho truchas grandes still ahead of us."

As we trudged upstream, Larry froze—

This is it, I thought. Nothing can stop this keen, voracious feeder from sipping in my dry fly. Everyone sensed it was a sure thing.

much like a heron about to stab a frog. Something was up. He turned slowly to us and addressed me.

"Have a look at this, Ollie. It's still your turn."

It was not really a pool but, rather, a peculiar run strewn with rocks. In one of the troughs was a magnificent rainbow of about seven pounds, hovering high in the current. Its demeanor was all nerves and bestial alertness as it quivered in the full current. It came up and took an insect with almost military deliberation.

This is it, I thought. Nothing can stop this keen, voracious feeder from sipping in my dry fly. Everyone sensed it was a sure thing.

I moved into position, assessed the distance,

appreciated the vagaries of the flow, pulled just the correct length of line from the reel, and commenced false-casting. I was precise and confident until, about three strokes into it, I came forward against solid resistance. My fly was hooked onto an immovable bristlecone pine.

Ever alert, Moe rushed in and freed the line. Cursing, and more careful now, I started to false-cast again but could no longer see the trout.

"Please," I whined to Larry, "tell me where to cast. I can't see the fish."

"He's gone. He saw the movement of you boys playing in the forest back here."

Somewhat soberly, we moved along through a dark avenue of ferns and tall redwoods. What a soft, damp peace there was on this side of the river. Clearly a thousand years meant nothing here, although, when I looked up and saw a vapor trail high overhead, I could feel the twenty-first century breathing hotly down our necks.

We had scanned a mile or so of the river, without seeing anything, when we arrived at an enormous and rather eccentric pool lying between two rocky cliffs.

Larry screamed, "It's a bloody ripper! My God! Careful, boys. Here, look through these palm fronds." We were plainly seeing a ten-pound trout and its slightly smaller mate nestled into their living room.

Technically, it was Curly's turn to fish. Unfortunately, a vicious wind had arisen and was gusting downriver, and these trout were in a terribly tough lie. It would take a long cast into the wind over slow-moving water, and we all knew, Curly most clearly of all, that he simply would never be able to make it.

Moe climbed down into position and waited for a lull in the wind. There wasn't any. It took repeated casts before Moe finally slipped one under the air. We had trouble seeing through the crinkled surface, but these fish were so big there were still their long, black forms, one of which turned and rushed downstream.

"Strike," screamed Larry, but it was too late. The fish had spit the fly out already. To boot, the one fish spooked the other, and both of them made a hasty trip in among the jumble of rocks ten yards upstream.

"Bastards," I heard Larry say as he pulled up his parka hood and started on his way. "We've got to break this streak."

"Well, how about you taking a turn then," I insisted. "We've never seen fish like these. You're not as nervous as we are. I'm not real sure anymore if we're operating with too much hair trigger or in Mexican overdrive."

Not surprisingly, the next pool had a good fish in the tail of it. Larry addressed the situation in a no-nonsense fashion. A very competent fly caster, he wasted no time in placing a small black nymph right in front of his target's nose. The target lunged and took. In the confusion that followed, the target elected to go over the riffle back downstream.

"I believe we'll get this one," Larry called out just a moment or two before the hook pulled out. There wasn't much else to do but laugh out loud together.

At this point we heard a yell from upstream. It was Curly, trying to tell us he'd found a real lunker feeding furiously right under his nose. We ran up the side of the river we were on, which was the opposite one from Curly. As we came abreast of him, we saw the fish immediately, a beautiful six-pounder literally slashing flies off the surface. Curly knew enough to get cracking, and it

was a piece of cake for him to cover the fish, which immediately grabbed his fly. Moe had sidled up to offer a little advice at his elbow.

It was a good pool in which to play a fish—not too deep, long, and uncomplicated by any obvious snags. And here was Curly, who had us worrying that he wasn't having a very pleasant day, firmly attached to the biggest trout of his life, a trout that looked as though it would be the first one landed by any of us.

Curly handled the job very well. He kept the pressure on while the rainbow ran first to the head of the pool, then clear to the tail. Moe, to his credit, did not badger Curly, but stood off behind him ready to help if needed. We were very pleased, because the weather was worsening and another such opportunity simply might not present itself. This fish would mean a lot to Curly, and I already had several good photos of him playing it.

Then the rainbow did a remarkable thing. It ran over to our side of the river, and rather calmly, we thought, circled a rock and broke Curly's leader. I would like to say we all felt worse than Curly did, but that was not the case.

"This is becoming damned serious," murmured Larry. "There are only three or four more pools before the falls. We mustn't be shut out."

The next pool was quite flat and shallow. Larry told me with all certainty that if we spotted a fish there, it would take a dry fly.

"A good, honest dry fly will change our luck," Larry stated.

Sure enough, a fish was there and rising. We agreed that Curly should be the one to fish. This trout looked like another beauty of five or six pounds.

Larry was right beside Curly, trying to forge

the event to a successful conclusion. After several failed tries, Curly landed his fly ahead of the fish, but too far to the right. The trout left its position anyway and executed a bizarre rolling, slow-motion take. In a moment of uncontrolled excitement, Curly whipped his fly rod back to strike and made one of the most depressing backcasts of his life.

Larry was losing his sense of humor. Perhaps he thought we were blaming him somehow for this ongoing comedy of errors. Maybe he thought Moe would punch him in the nose, or I might allow a grand piano to land somehow on his car, or Curly would slap him and twist his ear, making odd noises emanate therefrom.

There followed, then, five minutes of reassuring gibberish, about how fine it was just to have seen all this, how privileged we all felt to have been led to this most heavenly of rivers.

I stepped up to the next pool with a sense of weariness and resignation, two attitudes I secretly hoped would allow me to catch a fish by accident.

It didn't work. The trout we were fishing for was impossible for me to see, so I cast where Larry told me. He yelled, "Strike," and I did. Need I go on?

Larry gathered around us in a huddle. "Gentlemen, the last pool lies just ahead of us. Moe, you're in the gun seat. I have already seen a couple of rises up there. Put on this dry fly and try to think like a professional athlete."

The situation looked promising. The pool was simple and open, the current perfect, without any obvious treachery, and two trout were feeding aggressively. There was no need for Moe to be the least bit nervous just because this was our last chance and these trout were eight-pounders.

I must say that Moe delivered the goods. We all envied and admired his cast. The fly turned over perfectly even in the gale-force wind and started its jaunty ride on the current. It seemed like an hour before the fly rode over the fish's tail and left it like a tiny shuttle leaving a spacecraft. An odd thing happened then, still in excruciating slow motion.

The huge rainbow did a perfect about-face, raised its dorsal fin and part of its considerable back above the surface, and began cruising straight toward the little fly and, of course, toward the stunned Moe as well.

One seldom sees an eight-pound trout with a mouth the size of a boxer's right hand glower at you as he gulps in a glassful of water along with a Dan Bailey Royal Coachman. I'm convinced that anyone would have done what Moe did under the circumstances, which was to pull the fly directly out of the fish's mouth.

So, there you have it, the horse collar on the world's greatest trout stream. And even though at the outset we had all agreed to kill no fish in this river, even if we caught one the size of an Eletrolux vacuum cleaner, we had thirteen opportunities and muffed them all.

{excerpt}

Take my friends and my home—as an outcast I'll roam:
Take the money I have in the bank: It is just what I wish,
but deprive me of fish, and my life would indeed be a blank.

—Lewis Carroll, "The Two Brothers"

Caught Red Handed by Mike Robinson

It was 1941: I was a thirteen-year-old boy spending school holidays with three great-aunts and a great-uncle in a Victorian house in the south of England. My aunts were Quakers and very straight-laced and religious. Food rationing was beginning to bite and I was always hungry.

I had crept out of the house early that morning with a bamboo rod (that I had found in the attic) in hand and about thirty feet of cat-gut wrapped around it. For the past week I had been fishing with worms and grasshoppers in the river half a mile away, managing to catch three nice trout which were duly cooked and eaten in the woods.

On this particular morning I found a place under a bridge, well hidden by reeds, and with a worm on the hook I let all the gut line out to fish down a deep run. After a short time the rod was nearly wrenched out of my hands—the

game was on, a terrific battle which neither the fish nor I was about to give up. After seemingly ages I hauled this, to me, large fish into the shallows and onto a little beach where I picked up and clasped it to my chest with both hands.

It was then that I noticed a strong smell of pipe tobacco, and a voice bellowed, "Stay where you are, and don't move!" I turned around, rigid with fear, to face a stocky, red-faced, irate gentleman— it was my uncle Wolfred.

Without a word he strode forward, took the fish from my hands, gently unhooked it, waded into the water, held it in the current for a moment, and let it go.

"Don't look at me as if the world has fallen apart, young man. In fact you're damned lucky it was me who caught you. Do you have a license? Do you know this river is privately owned, and

is one of the best chalk streams in the country? You're lucky because, as it happens, I am acting warden for this seven-mile stretch of river, while all the young fellows are away at war."

I was quaking in my gumboots but noticed a gleam in his eye when he said, "I am going to punish you, and for the last week of your holidays you will come with me on my rounds, and you will keep up with me every inch of the way."

Uncle Wolfred's "rounds" meant fishing a couple of miles of river each day. What a punishment!

He had my full attention from the first; it was pure magic watching the fluid poetry of his fishing. He was a dry fly purist and wielded his ten-foot Hardy split cane rod as if it were no heavier than a knitting needle. On the fourth day, when he started me on casting, I needed both hands to handle it like a salmon rod. However, on the last day of the holidays I hooked my first trout on the fly, and the fish and I were both hooked for life.

The next summer holidays my uncle handed me a package. It comprised a seven-foot six-inch Hardy split cane fly rod, a reel, silk line and backing, a fly box and flies, and a box of gut casts. That was the beginning of a wonderful relationship between man, boy, and trout stream, one in which we were to learn a lot about life, each other, and ourselves in particular, for Uncle Wolfred was a philosopher who was close to nature and in tune with the infinite. I was to become his pupil and admirer for a number of years and as I grew older I appreciated more and more his consummate skills.

I later discovered his aging sisters regarded him as the "black sheep" of the family—he had made and lost two huge fortunes on the Manchester Cotton Exchange and at one time owned a yacht which he raced frequently, and once in

the America's Cup. It was not surprising that when the weather was unfishable he headed for the local pub at six o'clock and was often late for dinner.

I sometimes wonder how other people get started in fly fishing—those not lucky enough to be born near a trout stream.

Many years later when Uncle Wolfred was intent on getting me thoroughly inebriated at my stag party, he admitted that the cane rod I had found in the attic was his, when he was a boy. I have often wondered who taught him.

The love of angling increases with the lapse of years,
for its love grows by what it feeds on.

—JAMES HENSHALL, BOOK OF THE BLACK BASS

The Old Man by Nick Lyons

The old man was there when I came out of the woodline and into the clearing, when I turned the last corner. At first I smiled when I saw him casting from a chair perched on one of the wooden ramps. The Connetquot has dozens of these ramps and I do not like them. "That's the life," I thought, "but not for me."

Then I saw that the old man was sitting in a wheelchair, and that he held the lack line for his casts in his mouth.

I had walked briskly that bright, hot, autumn afternoon—the last day of the season—and sat down for a few moments to rest at one of the bench-tables near the hatchery. From where I sat I could see only the old man's right side and back. He was using a small bamboo rod and cast ably—his loops tight, his forward thrust authoritative—but not very far. I could not see his face, but I could tell by the way he leaned forward and studied the water that he was intent at his work.

And he was surely outfitted for the kill, with a long-handled net propped against the chair, an old wicker creel beside that, a full vest, and a khaki hat with a lamb's wool band crammed with bright flies.

I watched for ten minutes. He would cast across and slightly upstream, follow the fly down with head and rod, then pick up, false-cast once, and cast again. He was catching nothing.

I knew this stretch of what had once been the famous old Southside Club and now was run as a state park. The several hundred yards above the hatchery were reserved for the handicapped and aged. He'd earned it on both accounts. A neat little sign at the tail end of the run announced these restrictions. Once, several years ago, I came to the stretch from another road, for the first time, failed to see the sign, saw a dozen fish rising, and got an ego as big as the Ritz when I took just about all of them—and had to smile when I learned from

where. The few hundred yards of sap-green water contained hundreds of trout. You could see them holding over the light sand bottom between the lines of elodea, or they would bust out from the darker patches of waterweed—three, four at a time—to chase a fly. Too many fish. Far too many. They were hungry, too unselective. They lacked that critical eye without which gulling a fish becomes child's play.

The old man was catching none of them. His casts were true, and the pretty little stream is so small here that he could reach across it. Perhaps his fly picked up too much drag; perhaps he used too large a fly; perhaps the water held fewer trout than the day I fished it. It was the last day of the season: maybe the fish had seen enough artificials and would starve before they'd chase another. I don't know. I rather wanted him to catch a trout. I rather wanted to see him play and land one. Then I would get on with my own affairs, those I had come for, the last rites of not an especially productive season.

Lulled by the quiet of the place and the warm afternoon, tired from my rush to get there, I leaned on an arm, watched the old man, and amused myself imagining this feeble old sport as a young man. I stayed longer than I thought I would. Had he been a member of this club? Had he once fished the four-mile length of it, each run and pool of it? Did he resent being condemned to this one rather privileged spot, on a ramp? Did the river's new public role disturb him? Did he resent newcomers and plebians like me and wooden ramps and the death of an old order? He was old enough —in his late seventies at least—to have fished in the twenties and thirties. What fabulous fishing he might have known! He might have known and fished with Hewitt and LaBranche and Jennings.

He might have fished . . . well, anywhere; he might have caught wild trout in rivers that are polluted or madly crowded now, that were ruined before I saw my first fly. Had he been vigorous and adventuresome once? Had he pioneered new waters? Had he been truly exceptional at this game, one of those private, unheralded masters at it—a man quite as good as the experts, and I have known a few, but quite uninterested in the public or commercial aspects of the sport? He certainly cast with distinction, though not far and not consistently well. Even his right arm creaked, hitched, failed to follow through. He was a very old man. Twice his fly slapped on the water. Once it hit an overhanging branch and luckily came free. Had he been disappointed, discouraged to the point of despair, when his body betrayed him? Who brought him here? A son perhaps. Maybe an abler, younger friend. Someone he had once fished beside, as an equal. He was dependent now, tethered to those who could and would help, a burden, an inconvenience. Were they condescending? Did they pity him? And what had happened to his body? A stroke? An accident? And how long ago? His left hand appeared to move not at all; I could see that his legs were pinched together, thin under bulky pants, lifeless. Had he though when all this happened that it was at last over for him— wading swift streams, tying cunning flies, pursuing sport and mystery and independence and perhaps, like me, his soul in moving water? Perhaps. And perhaps not. He might have been paralyzed fifty years ago, or thirty years ago, or after he retired; he might even have started to fly fish after this mangling of his body took place. Fly fishing in this fashion, as he now practiced it, might be the only kind he knew, his salvation. But I did not think so. There was something too intent in his

manner, his gestures, too skillful in his cast. The man had once been a superb fly fisherman. And when you have once done something well, quite as finely and purely as you are able, there must be a deep humiliation in being reduced to a state such as this. Once his eyes might have seen the quick, bright wink of a trout underwater, on the far side of the river. Once he could fish all day, on any man's river, from first light until the hushed gray of dusk. Once he could fit a 7X leader point through the eye of a #20 fly the first time he tried. Once he could tie midges, wrap rods, move lithely in a river, become one with it. Once. Had he slipped slowly over the years, so slowly he could not feel the fine edge vanish? Was this to be his last time out, a final trip, a last fling at it before a winter he might not survive? Had he stopped liking to go out—worn down by the cruelty of expectations, the blunders, the memories? How much did he hurt from being unable to do what once he had done with such delight, what now he was reduced to practice crudely and in the tamest of places?

I could not see his face. I could not tell.

Now and again he leaned perilously forward to get an extra foot or two to his cast. He strained. Then he put his fly firmly into an overhanging branch. He pulled the line taut with his mouth, grasped the line with his rod hand, pointed the rod and the place where it was hooked, and pulled straight back. He could not do it. On his third try I found myself rising from my seat to help him. On his fourth try the leader broke.

Then he retrieved line, brought the leader to his mouth, leaned the rod against the chair, secured a fly box and, out of my sight, fumbled for ten minutes before he was ready to fish again. He appeared now to have some little use of his left

hand. Once he raised it—clawed and crabbed— and held the fly to the light. Before he cast, he let the fly hang loose from the propped-up rod, cupped his right hand under his right leg and raised the leg and repositioned it a few inches to one side.

I went off then, restless as always, brooding, making up fantastic stories, remembering the boy I once was, barefoot in a mountain creek as clear as truth, as cold as snow.

As always, I was glad to be on the water. I piddled here and there and found a few large brookies camped under a long willow branch and coaxed them out; I made some blunders you'd have thought impossible; and, after the sun had vanished and the sky was merely bright gray, I returned to clean my few fish on the bench-table near the hatchery.

I had forgotten the old man.

He was there on the ramp. But now his rod was sharply bent. Twenty-five feet downstream a heavy brook trout rolled and pocked the surface. The old man held his rod high and the arc grew sharper. Then the fish turned. Then, in a few minutes, I could see the white of it on the surface, and the man was transferring the rod to his crabbed left hand, supporting it between his legs. For a moment he faltered. I found myself rising to help him. Then he grasped the long-handled net with his right hand, lowered it, and scooped up the fish.

It was a pretty brookie, all right—plump, bright, about seventeen inches.

"Bravo," I said softly. "Well done, old man."

And then he turned, still holding his trout in the net; he turned, looked around him, saw me, held his trout a bit higher, and smiled. I saw his eyes. I looked closely, beyond the crabbed body, at his eyes. His eyes, large and bright behind thick glasses, were smiling, too.

*While we are not yet legions, we are more than a handful. We are no longer
the girlfriend or wife who picks up a rod and wades only for her partner's benefit.
We are there because we like to fish and are serious about it.*

—Margot Page, *Little Rivers*

From Reel Women by Lyla Foggia

In 1895, the first woman was observed fly fishing in the Catskills in upstate New York in the companionship of Theodore Gordon, who is credited as the founder of the American school of dry-fly fishing. According to Austin M. Francis in *Catskill Rivers: Birthplace of American Fly Fishing*, "She wore a tam-o'-shanter, sweater, short jacket, and skirts, with stout shoes and leggings. . . . As she fished, her long skirts caressed the ripples, creating the illusion that she moved along on the surface of the stream." Francis also relates that even though this mysterious woman broke Gordon's heart, he later said of her: "The best chum I ever had in fishing was a girl, and she tramped just as hard and fished quite as patiently as any man I ever knew."

Francis also provides us with Fred White's enlightening reminiscences, recorded in 1923, of observing women fly fishers in the Catskills since the turn of the century:

"I remember distinctly the first woman at Beaverkill to put on boots and, even with a knee length skirt, dare to brave the disapproval of the porch sitters at Davidson's. It simply wasn't done and she came pretty near being regarded as fast as the water that rippled about her knees. Now the river is full of 'em and they don't bother with skirts either. And they catch fish—some of them—and big ones, too. Whether you like it or not the women are here to stay in trout fishing as on the golf course and at the ballot box, and when all is said and done, I believe it to be an excellent thing—for the women. They can wear my second best waders anytime."

[excerpt]

Circles on the Water by Margot Page

When I was growing up in Connecticut, my maternal grandparents were passionate about some weird adult thing called "fly fishing," a recreation in which they wore an embarrassing (to my adolescent '60s eyes) attire of fat wading pants, bosomy khaki vests and odd hats with hair hooks stuck in them.

Instead of resembling the other yacht-club side of my family, these two elders actually *liked* clambering around the banks of a river in all sorts of weather, pursuing fish and telling the inevitable big fish stories.

How odd, rare, and wonderful for me now—thirty years later—to be married to a fly-fishing maniac. Tom and I—like my grandfather and grandmother—also spend months every year crawling over rocks, marveling at the evanescent colors of a wild trout and brandishing our own versions of fishing tales, which, at this point in our lives, usually revolve around how women and men work out equal opportunity in a male-dominated sport.

When I was a girl, I was aware that my grandfather was distantly famous for a book he had written. Published when he was nearly eighty years old, *Fishless Days, Angling Nights* cemented his place in the little universe of angling. A man with many names, he wrote under the pen name Sparse Grey Hackle; our family called him "Deac";

his real name was Alfred Waterbury Miller.

A city boy "by birth and breeding," a student who was once a debating champion of Greater New York, my grandfather described fishing at night as "a gorgeous gambling game in which one stakes the certainty of long hours of faceless fumbling, nerve-wracking starts, frights, falls and fishless baskets against the off chance of hooking into . . . a fish as long and heavy as a railroad tie and as unmanageable as a runaway submarine."

He wrote about a five-mile section of the Neversink River in New York's Catskill region as "a place of rugged bristling steeps, moss-hung rock faces, brawling rapids and deep blue pools. So wild . . . that one expected any moment to see the painted, feathered head of a Mohawk rise stealthily among the alders."

When this glorious landscape was bulldozed into desolation to prepare for the Neversink Reservoir, Deac told how he wandered across the "barren desecrated ground" stripped of familiar landmarks and heard the sound of running water. Sticking out of the baked mud was the pipe from the spring that had fed the cellar of his old fishing camp, from which poured "a strong, lively stream, clear as air and cold as ice, the only living thing in that valley of silent ruin."

He drank of it deeply and finally and so said farewell to his Golden Age of Angling.

Although he lived to be almost ninety-one, Deac didn't live long enough for us to fish together. Fishing instruction had been offered only to the male grandchildren in my family and, besides, as a teenager I was far more interested in boys and trying to straighten my unfashionably curly hair.

And by the time I married the fly-fishing nut who initiated me into the sport, it was too late for Deac and me.

But not so for me and my grandmother, although almost. An indomitable, jaunty, round woman who bustled with birdlike, girlish energy, my grandmother was eighty-six years old the first time I fished with her. Because of her dauntless prowess and long history of fishing with him on Catskill rivers, Deac had long ago christened her "Lady Beaverkill."

When my grandmother and I went fishing together for the first time, I had, to date, received only rather impatient angling instruction from my new husband (apparently I had used up most of his patience on our first outing) and was still at the stage of nervous struggles with tangles of lines and hooks that caught on every bush, tree, and blade of timothy.

That day in August 1986 my grandmother smoothly strung up her rod, stepped energetically into her old patched waders—they must have been at least thirty years old and were belted, if I remember correctly, with a frayed twine-and-bandana arrangement—and with a twinkly pride in her mastery and an obvious joy at being on the stream again, she stepped into the river to cast crisply, calmly, beautifully.

We fished a marble-lined stream that runs through one of Vermont's most fertile farmscapes—a valley of historic farms and houses bordered by undulating, lush mountains, where, during the early spring hatches, the heady smell of manure from the farmers' cornfields curls the nose. She exulted in the appearance of even the most modest of trout and chanted softly in her melodic, light voice, "Here fishy, fishy, heeere fishy, fishy." . . .

One evening, on the same river, I watched as birds swooped over her head through the insect hatches and the last rays of sunlight gilded the tips of the firs and maples that lined the water and towered above her. In the twilight, she held Tom's hand as they waded over the slippery rocks, the dark waters ringing out in concentric circles from their careful steps, the occasional bat darting above them like a little flying shadow.

She caught a small rainbow and played him proudly—rather longer than necessary—reluctant to let go of the moment, the evening, the cold clasp of the water around her legs and the tug of a shimmering wild thing at the end of her line. . . .

It was not many months afterward that a knee and then a wrist gave out and the new Orvis hip boots she finally treated herself to—and had worn perhaps twice since—were retired. She was the only woman I knew who honestly preferred to hear—and tell—fishing tales above anything else and she continued to tell and listen to such stories until the end of her life. . . .

I miss both my grandparents, now, when I go to the water. I miss exploring the thread that has connected us through time, genes, geography, and circumstance of birth. What would it have been like to stand proudly next to my grandfather on the banks of a shining river of water, as I did—finally—with my grandmother?

{excerpt}

The outdoor life pleased these old men
because they believed any properly obsessed fly fisherman
carried rivers and trout inside him.

—Harry Middleton, *The Earth Is Enough*

Grandpa's Fish by Greta Gaines

What to do when a fish morphs from gills and guts into something larger—a memory that splashes across three generations of anglers, alternating between dream and reality? Born to my grandfather, this fish swam through my father Charles and landed with me. Even before I hooked her one cool April morning on Georgia's Soquee River, I dreamt of her—a big rainbow on a light line.

When dad woke me at seven a.m., I was mad. I'd overheard him moments earlier talking to my mother in our shared cabin at the Brigadoon Lodge. He was telling her that someone had already come back from the river and had caught a ten-pound rainbow. I confronted him but he said I was nuts.

"Your mother's asleep and no one's been to the river," he said. "Now get up."

My grandfather was never more alive than when he was fly fishing. Hooking an eight-inch brookie got the same feverish response as an eighty-pound tarpon. "Hot damn!" he'd yell— and those were the first words out of my mouth when that hefty rainbow hit my fly and crashed through the small pool she was laid up in.

The tiny reel flew off the rod, I went over my head in the river after it, and the guides and my father came running down the bank toward my screams. With no reel, and the line in my left hand, it looked like I didn't have a chance to land her. But twenty minutes of graceless fighting led that rainbow to the net and I was sick with elation. They said she might have been some kind of Georgia state record, but none of that mattered to me. It was just grandfather's fish coming back through the rod, through the dream, through the glory of that southern morning.

Osgood as It Gets by Bob Ripley

Columbus Day weekend 2004 was the very last time Dad and I fished together. My thoughtful wife Cheryl hatched the idea to share our long weekend in the Adirondacks with my parents. It turned out to be a memorable, almost magical trip.

We reserved a modern log home on Osgood Pond (Osgood as it gets!) in the northwest corner of the Park. The weather in the Adirondacks at this time of year can be dicey. Snow is not uncommon in these higher altitudes. But we had four of the most spectacular autumn days one could imagine. Crisp clear mornings greeted us every day with afternoon temperatures in the seventies, above normal for the season. Though past peak, most of the hardwoods still held their leaves, with bright ochres and rust colors predominant.

Loons greeted our arrival at Osgood Pond with their beautiful eerie calls. It was a good omen. The camp was situated on a bluff with a forty-step descent to the lake and dock. We had to caution Dad, who at eighty-four years young would skip down the log staircase at an alarming pace. I

think he was showing Wanda that he was still a young stud. Once at the pond, which was really more of a lake, you were greeted by a spectacular mountain vista which was doubled in a watery mirror almost every morning and evening.

We all felt at home in the comfortable rental camp. It had every amenity, including a Jacuzzi. And to add to the sense of home, we cooked most of our meals, including some of Dad's healthy favorites: macaroni and cheese, pork chops, popcorn, and, of course, fresh pan-fried trout. In order to have that fish fry, we had to catch them. Dad and I had fooled around with the pond's abundant perch supply, but trout were what we were really after. So we left the girls at camp with their reading and bird watching and set out for the nearby Saranac River, promising to return at a decent hour. As any fisherman knows, it's hard to predict exact return times.

As we traveled the twenty-odd miles to the Saranac, Dad reminisced about Adirondack trips he'd made as a young man. I'd heard them all

before, but it was good to hear yet again about the fishing trip to Onchiota, when all the guys chipped in two dollars apiece for gas money, only to be savaged by blackflies when they arrived. Some of the crew were under the mistaken impression that they'd be meeting girls on the trip, but there were none for miles. And he also retold the time that he hiked into the High Falls at Wanakena with Chuck Helsing. Somehow, I never tired of those old stories.

I knew exactly where I wanted to take Dad that day in October. I wanted to put him in a spot where he could work his magic with his salted minnows and not have to fight the river's stronger currents. The old iron bridge at Pup Hill Road seemed like the perfect spot. There was a good set of rapids that fed the immense pool below the bridge where Dad could cover a lot of water without much wading. I wished him luck and headed for the tailout.

I'd barely reached my spot when I noticed Dad's rod bent in a familiar arc. Seeing him net the first fish of the day a few minutes later gave me more satisfaction than I'd felt on a stream in a long time. Struggling to hide my emotions, I shouted, "Nice going, Dad!" This was going to be a very good day indeed! Dad added two more healthy brown to his creel—icing on the cake. I added to the fish fry using a dry fly/nymph dropper rig, but I felt a twinge of guilt when I took a large brown downstream of where he was fishing. How I wished that he had caught that hard-fighting fish.

He tried to hide it, but I couldn't help but notice the difficulty he was having wading even in the calm shallow areas of the stream. I saw a fear in his eyes, a fear of falling, that I'd never seen before in the fifty years we'd fished together.

As he teetered in the shadows, I tried to help him save face by blaming his rubber hip boots, saying he should have the better-gripping felt-soled kind. But I could see he was failing. Probably the early symptoms of the cancer that would take him from us only six months later.

We had enough trout for dinner, but I wanted him to sample one more spot before we returned to camp. A Saranac tributary, Cold Brook (not to be confused with the Jungle) was on our way back to Osgood Pond, and I knew he would find comfortable wading there in a small, familiar-sized stream. I didn't even string up my fly rod, just content to be his guide on this beautiful little brook.

Unfortunately, the stream was flush with fallen leaves, snagging his hooks and probably unnerving the trout. But at the last pool we fished, Dad enticed a pan-sized brookie to take his minnow. He held the pretty fish in his hand for my inspection. It was a classic Adirondack native: a dark back with brilliant golden vermiculations, and bright blue and red spots on its sides.

For some reason, I felt a strong desire to capture the moment and snuck my camera out of my vest without him knowing it. "Smile," I said as I snapped the picture the moment he straightened up from washing his hands in the stream. Little did I know that that photo would be the last one I would ever take of him, and would grace his memorial service the following spring.

That evening we enjoyed a trout feast at camp, and everyone commented that the fish tasted especially good. It was a special day, fishing with my dad on a perfect autumn afternoon in the beautiful Adirondack mountains. And I think now how appropriate it was that the very last fish Dad caught in his life was a brook trout.

And, God bless him, he released it.

The Fishing Car by John Gierach

When I was a young feller, I thought my Uncle Leonard had invented the concept of the fishing car, the elderly but still serviceable vehicle that was reserved for angling and angling-related activities to the extent that it was kept loaded, like the shotgun behind the kitchen door. But then I thought Leonard had invented a lot of things, some of which have since turned out to be among the oldest jokes in the world. It's understandable, I guess. In matters pertaining to fishing—not to mention farming, guitar playing, and a number of other things—he had the authority that comes from experience; and I was also into a bit of adolescent hero worship.

The idea of the fishing car spoke to me of a way of life. It was the thought that you could be a sportsman in the same way you could be a Baptist or a farmer or a blond; that being a fisherman could be as much a part of your identity as your fingerprints. And I was at the age where I had just started to puzzle over my identity.

The fishing car in those days was the "ambler." It had actually once said "Rambler" in chrome letters on the hood, but a minor run-in with a fence post had resulted in the abbreviated version.

Of course, there was no thought of having it fixed.

It was a black station wagon with many thousands of miles on it that somehow always ran—after a little prodding—and that was always stocked with axes, minnow, buckets, tackle boxes, rods, etc. The upholstery was ragged, the windshield was pitted, the dashboard was dusty, the tires were fair, and it had an aroma about it of beer, Coke, cleaned fish, wet wool, and a few other things that were hard to place. The exact opposite of that new car smell.

I don't know what ever happened to it, but, by all rights, it should have been bronzed and placed on a pedestal on the banks of a good bass pond somewhere in Indiana.

I spent as much time as I could with Leonard while I was growing up, and much of it passed in the front seat of the ambler following lazy, circuitous routes to one bass pond or another. We drove the dirt roads most of the time. Some were so little used that by midsummer the tall grass growing between the wheel ruts would slap the front bumper. The roads in those rural counties were laid out more or less on grids, and we got to where we were going by starting at a

known point and then angling in what seemed like the right direction.

In the course of things we discovered several little towns that were doubtless unknown to the outside world; towns so slowly paced that a dog could safely sleep on the warm pavement of Main Street in the late afternoon, because everyone knew that Butch might be taking a nap in the road in front of the hardware store. Butch himself, a fair-to-middling hunting dog in his younger years, could live to the ripe age of eighteen or twenty, and when he finally passed away—quietly, in his sleep—the whole town would feel bad about it for a day or two.

Sometimes we'd stop and ask directions, which could be a laborious process. Everyone knew where everything was, but what was County Road 23 to us was usually the Road Out to the Jones Place to everyone else. I never saw Leonard use a store-bought map, but we followed several that were scratched on paper napkins or matchbook covers.

Leonard was a master at navigating in farm country, but we did occasionally get lost. This was known as "taking the scenic route." There were rare times when we never quite got to where we were going, but we always got somewhere.

Leonard made a point of appearing confident and in charge, so it was difficult to tell when he knew where he was and when he didn't. There were times when I'd have sworn we were hopelessly lost, but then we'd pull up to an unlocked gate that looked exactly like the last twenty unlocked gates we'd passed, and he would describe the pond that was still out of sight down a two-wheel dirt track: its size, its shape, the muddy bank, the cattails along the east side, everything. Of course, he did have the reputation of knowing where every bass and most of the panfish in three counties lived.

He also knew half the people in the same area, and if he didn't know them, he soon would. He was deeply in touch with the interlocking networks of relations, work, church, and grange that tied the farming community together, and all he needed to make a connection was a name off a mailbox.

It was something to see. Leonard would bounce the ambler up a perfectly strange driveway, negotiate through the dogs, find the owner (who was invariably poking at some broken piece of machinery), and deftly establish himself as a neighbor, if not an out-and-out friend of the family. There would then follow an interminable period of fence leaning, gravel kicking, sky squinting, and a rambling philosophical discussion that included everything from the hound dog at your feet to the President of the United States. Of the two, the dog was the more competent.

It took time, but sooner or later we'd end up catching large bass from an obscure pond that hadn't been fished five times in as many years. The farmer always got some cleaned fish out of it, and then we'd pile into the ambler and drive off, waving at a man who was now our friend or who, at the very least, was too polite to say no to a couple of nice enough guys.

Driving home at night it would occur to me that, although life would surely provide some interruptions, there'd be nothing wrong with doing this all the time.

Of all the trips Leonard and I took in that car, the one I remember most clearly was our longest and last. My family had moved to Minnesota, and I hadn't seen Leonard in a while. . . .

It so happened that my sister decided to get married one summer not long after we'd moved to Minnesota, a state that was full of lakes which

were, in turn, lousy with fish. Weeks before the actual festivities, the family began to gather. By the time Leonard and Aunt Dora arrived, the house was filled with grannies and aunts and mobs of cousins on the way.

Leonard and I got together out in the backyard, where it was quiet, and decided the best thing for us to do was go wet a line somewhere, just to get out from underfoot, you understand. We packed quickly, left quietly, and drove north in the ambler.

We drove for some eighteen or twenty hours, watching the landscape go from fields to scattered groves to coniferous forests and feeling the hot closeness of the summer air become cool and sharply scented with pine. Somewhere along the line we turned off the main highway onto a dirt country road.

Up there the roads were fewer and farther between than in rural Indiana and anything but straight. They didn't seem to go much of anywhere, but all roads go somewhere, and we finally pulled up to a medium-sized lake with tree-lined banks and water lilies as if it had been our destination from the start. We rented a small, rickety cabin that came with an equally small and rickety rowboat. Both leaked, but were thoughtfully equipped with the appropriate tin cans.

In the days that followed, we caught fish.

There were foot-long perch in the little bay right outside the cabin door that came into the boat with the kind of regularity you somehow only remember from long ago. On the first night we sat down to baked beans from a can and a platter of breaded and fried perch fillets from a lake that neither of us had seen or even heard of before. Definitely the way to begin a fishing trip.

We took smallmouth bass from around the rocky points on small floating lures and spoons. They were an olivish-bronze color and jumped the way I would later learn the rainbow trout do.

The northern pike came from deeper water to big, heavy Johnson's Weedless Spoons trailing strips of pickled pork rind. They were my favorites, being large, prehistorically ugly, and—by stretching the imagination some—even a little dangerous. Leonard said the real fight with a big pike began when you got him in the boat. In any case, there were some minor injuries, complete with blood, and I loved it.

During the middle of some days, we drove around the back roads to look at other lakes and talk to sellers of bait and renters of boats, all of whom were getting their share of fish that week. "Getting our share" is one of those wonderful fishing euphemisms that sound promising, but that can mean damn near anything.

As I said, Leonard was a great raconteur of the fence-leaning or one-foot-up-on-the-dock-piling school, and he enjoyed talking and joking with fishermen as much as he liked fishing itself. He was good at it, too. He knew that few fishermen, himself included, would tell a stranger what he needed to know straight out, so he assembled information not so much by the facts as by evaluating the empty space around them. He taught me, for example, not to pay attention to the lures that were well stocked, regardless of how pretty they were or how hard the sales pitch was, but to always ask what had once hung on the empty pegs. The ones that were sold out were the ones that caught fish.

I guess it took me a long time to come to appreciate the charms and real advantages of just talking about fishing, looking at water, leaning on things, reading between the lines. At the time I was a little impatient. You remember, it was childhood; the days of wooden rowboats when men who didn't know each other could stand and chew the fat for hours. But I knew I'd be doing it myself someday, so I paid attention and mostly kept my mouth shut in the borrowed style of the strong, silent type. The compliment I was being paid was that of being left to myself—of not having to be watched and kept amused. Back home I felt like a man who was being treated like a boy. Out fishing with Leonard, it was the other way around.

Then, as now, these conversations tended to dissolve around late afternoon when the first boils could be seen out along the weed beds. There was a slow, satisfying logic about it all.

I drove the ambler on many of those back roads, not because I was allowed to, as I'd been in the past, but because a fishing partner shares the driving chores. Never mind that I was too young to have a license.

It wasn't until a few hours before the wedding —not quite the last possible moment—that we strolled in the back door sublimely unconcerned, wearing clothes we'd fished in for a week and carrying armloads of fillets. The house was in a uniform state of hysteria: the women were all at a dead run or off in a corner weeping, while the men were looking mounted in suits that had last been worn at funerals. I've since come to recognize the pained, furtive look they wore as symptomatic of the powerful need for a drink.

"It's about time," someone said, and we were grabbed by the ears and forcibly washed. The story is told that our clothes had to be burned, but that may be an exaggeration. I've never felt less welcome arriving at an event I was supposed to attend.

I remember coming downstairs to the kitchen all clean and dressed up and running into Dad.

He'd been stuffed into a tuxedo and was fondling a big glass of bourbon with a single, lonely ice cube floating in it. We were alone, but the sound of chattering washed in from the front room.

"Caught some fish," Dad said (not a question).

"Yup," I answered, all puffed up with teenage conceit and vanity.

He raised his glass slightly in a toast and flashed me an evil little grin, something between envy, pride, and resignation. Now that I think about it, maybe he did see the humor in it now and then, or if not the humor, then something. Dad always tried to be strict and straight-laced with me, but word around the family was he'd had his moments as a young man. I remember wanting to tell him I'd driven the car for hundreds of miles, and then thinking I'd best not push my luck. . . .

I guess my sister got married okay that summer, although I can't say I actually remember the ceremony. All the fish got eaten, and Leonard and I were eventually forgiven, though I've never been quite sure what for.

When it was all over, I walked Leonard and Aunt Dora out to the fishing car. They were headed back to Indiana, and the ambler didn't look right with suitcases and garment bags in it. Leonard and I ran down some brief, vague plans for future fishing trips, and then, with nothing left to say, they drove off. As it turned out, I would never see the ambler again, and Leonard and I would never fish together again, either, although I didn't know that at the time. You never know those things at the time.

The last time I saw it, the car was still dusty from the trip to the lake. Aunt Dora had wanted to have it washed, but there just wasn't time.

[excerpt]

Love the Man, Love the Fly Rod by Allison Moir-Smith

The meandering Ruby River—pebbly riffles where smaller fish thrive, sharply cut curves and deep, clear pools where larger fish live—is the perfect stage on which to show off. It's never deeper than I can handle, never threatening to take me down. This is my graduation, I suppose, from this summer of fishing. Fish are jumping like popcorn in a pan, and John is behaving like an overexcited Little League coach.

"Come on, catch him. Just float the fly down right in front of his nose . . . No! Not there, you'll scare him . . . Good. Good. Good. Too much arm . . . Careful of the rod tip . . . "

"*You* take the goddamn rod!" I spit back.

"No! I am going to watch you *catch that fish.*"

On my third cast, my Blue-Winged Olive lands at the head of the deep pool ten feet ahead of the big brown. The current kicks it out of his feeding lane, but I give it some action—a few quick jerks—and it goes back in the drift. My coach behind me inhales loudly and holds his breath as the fly passes over the fish. It takes my fly and runs, heading toward a thicket of dead branches. "Rod tip up! Rod tip up!" he yells, but it's already up.

I reel in the fish gently. John laughs as I coax it, saying, "Come here, sweet, sweet." I wet my hand and pick up the fish, its sunset orange spots glinting in the bright sun. Water purls around me as I bend down to tug the barbless hook from his pink mouth and hold him facing upstream to force oxygen back into his system. Then I set him free, releasing this wonderful, wild creature as old as the Ice Age, back into the cycle of nature.

I look back at my Big Sweetie, who is grinning in a way I had never seen before. "I really love you," he says quietly.

We spend the afternoon in a quiet dance, leapfrogging each other from pool to pool about three-quarters of a mile upstream. He fishes one pool his way, I fish the next, mine. I feel like I've attained the Zen plateau that is the core of the fly-fishing experience. But my serene state, I realize, is due more to the experience of fly fishing as a shared event; as I reel in my fifth fish, he gives me a thumbs-up from a pool upstream.

{excerpt}

From Black Gnat by John England

I recall, in a haze of blue sky and yellow tussock-covered hill, many mornings on Lake Sheppard, but few individual moments come to mind. The incident I most remember actually occurred on adjoining Lake Katrine, a lake of slightly larger proportions, and in the afternoon. It was in December 1954 and we had fished Lake Sheppard in the morning with little success. At that stage of my career I had caught several fish of three pounds or so but had failed to land any larger fish, probably because patience was not my greatest virtue.

That afternoon my father decided not to venture to the Lake Sumner outlet but to visit two business acquaintances who were camping on the edge of Lake Katrine. Both men were in their sixties and had been fishing all their lives. It was well into the afternoon when we arrived at the campsite, a time when the fish were generally inactive, and consequently both fishermen were recovering in their tent from the exertions of the morning. My father's arrival prompted renewed vigor, and the extraction of a bottle of whisky. The invitation to partake of this reviving liquid was greeted with much favor by my father, but his fourteen-year-old son found the excitement difficult to understand. Surprisingly there was little wind, the sky was clear, and there might well be a fish on the move. Why sit in a tent for any purpose?

Many times in later years I have possibly missed a potential trophy for the same reason, but not that afternoon. I excused myself, walked to the lake edge, and within minutes noted a fish feeding well within casting distance, perhaps fifty yards around the small bay in which the camp was sited. I watched the fish's beat for several minutes and concluded with mounting excitement that it was a large fish. Using the standard method I cast well ahead of the fish's apparent path, crouched low in the water to conceal my presence, and waited. A gentle inshore breeze caused the fly to drift back to the lake edge, as I cautiously took up the slack in the line. The fish was rising methodically but sporadically, heading in my general direction. Fortunately it appeared to be closer to the shore than I had originally thought, but when my fly drifted to within fifteen feet of my position I decided I should cast again. Just as I was about to lift the fly from the water, the fish rose within twenty feet of me

and seconds later my Cock-y-bondhu disappeared as a large snout slowly emerged and dropped back under the surface. I waited momentarily, then tightened my line. The reel screamed. So far, so good.

Fighting a fish on light fly gear is comparable only to fighting a large fish in a substantial fast-flowing river when the fish decides to leave its home area and run downstream. Often in a river or stream the fish will stay close to base of its own volition, or can be encouraged to run upstream at reasonably close quarters. Not so in a lake, where there is no reason for the fish not to flee as far as possible from the source of irritation and obvious danger. That afternoon my line disappeared to reveal the backing on my reel several times, but each time the fish stopped its run before the end of the backing. Each time it was slowly coaxed back to shore; and each time the run was weaker.

Meanwhile back in the tent more than one whisky had been consumed, but some flash of insight suggested to my father and his friends that there must be some good reason for my failure to reappear within minutes. They set out to locate me, now several hundred yards along the shore, saw me in the distance, and quickly realized I had hooked a good fish. Glasses in hand, they appeared behind me and within seconds proffered more advice than I had received since my first fly-fishing trip on the North Branch several years before. Happily, by now advice was unnecessary as the fish was clearly close to exhaustion and was ready for netting.

Netting. With horror I realized I had left my net back at the tent, and my newfound advisors had come with their hands otherwise full. A net was essential, for the lake had a steep bank at least three feet high for several hundred yards in either direction, but the fish might well break free while a net was obtained from the tent. Always a man of decision, my father, mentally refreshed by his sojourn in the tent, had the answer almost immediately. He was wearing a polo neck jersey which would be more than adequate. The jersey was removed, the sleeves carefully knotted, and my father took up an appropriate position in the water at the lake's edge. With trembling care I maneuvered the fish over the jersey, now upturned under the water. In triumph my father raised the jersey skyward. I can still see the look of horror on his face as he realized he had failed to knot the neck of the jersey. I can still feel my own despair.

Having been exposed, if briefly, to fresh air, the fish found new life. It careered toward the center of the lake, the line running with surprising freedom through the jersey which my father continued to hold open. Clearly there was no way of knotting the neck at that stage. To be fair, that fish deserved freedom, but miraculously the hook held and eventually the fish was wound back to the bank. My father was not to be thwarted. He dived on the completely exhausted fish like a lion on its prey and emerged, soaking, but with the fish firmly in his grasp.

For my father and his friends it was cause for great celebration. At least a further dram was appropriate. For me it was a matter of quiet elation. I needed no whisky. I had landed, if with some unusual assistance, a brown trout of excellent proportions weighing close to five pounds. To date that was my best fish by far.

{excerpt}

Fishermen are born honest,
but they get over it.

—ED ZERN, *To Hell With Fishing*

Charity on the Little South by Ernest Schwiebert

The cooking smells of eggs and fresh trout and coffee drifted through the tent. There is a half-hour in the morning when a sleeping bag has an almost delicious warmth. It ends when the sun gets hotter, playing its leafy patterns of light on the canvas.

You awake? asked my father.

Yes, I answered deep in the goose down. You fish the early hatch this morning? I yawned sleepily.

It was pretty good, he said. Smell them?

I laughed and yawned again. The best fish went about fifteen inches, he said.

Good fish, I said. Where'd he take?

Forks Pool, he answered.

We were camped on the Little South two hundred yards above its junction with the Pere Marquette. It was our annual trip to Michigan when school sessions were over, and it was our first morning on the river that summer. The breakfast utensils were washed and scoured in the current, and we rigged our tackle.

We walked down the road along the river.

Who's fishing? said my father.

There was an old Plymouth parked near the bridge. Damn! I said. They're fishing the water we wanted!

There was a man in working clothes fishing a night-crawler in the run above a tangle of logs. His two sons were fishing worms downstream, working their bait under the bushes.

They would be in our favorite water, I grumbled.

Maybe we can Tom Sawyer them, said my father.

You really think so? I grinned. Talk them into fishing another piece of water? My father laughed softly.

Let's give it a try, he said.

We walked down to where they were fishing. Had any luck? we asked. Nothing, the man answered.

It's not good morning water, my father said.

No? He looked puzzled.

You have to stand right over them to fish bait here,
father explained. It spooks the fish to get too close.

That so? He reeled in his night-crawler.

It's good dry-fly water, my father continued,
but there's better worming over at Baldwin.

Where at Baldwin? The man waved to his sons.

Try the fish-hatchery stretch, I suggested. There's
a deep concrete channel between the spillways.

That's right, added my father.

Those fish are used to seeing people, I continued, and there're some big browns there. That
part was true because we had seen them ourselves,
and once I had hooked a heavy fish and played it
for an hour before the fly suddenly pulled out.

We'll try it, said the workman. We're obliged!

They started the battered Plymouth and drove
north into town, and the boys waved. It worked!
We grinned guiltily at each other and walked
down toward the river.

It was a good morning. There was a fine hatch
of caddis-flies, and the trout were already rising
well. We both took several good fish, and were
fishing the still tree-sheltered stretch of the Little
South where the man and his sons had fished
when a car stopped on the road. It was the same
battered Plymouth.

Hey mister! yelled the boys.

Their father came around the car. Sure want
to thank you folks! he grinned. Can't thank you
enough!

My father looked at me, and we stood in the
river with the current sliding past our waders.
What do you suppose they want now?

Are they serious? I whispered.

The workman went to his trunk. Yessir! He
raised it and dragged out a thirty-inch brown.
Caught this eight-pounder right where you said!
he laughed. Can't thank you enough!

On the Divide by Nick Lyons

"You really took five and lost a big one?" the boy said as we sat at the linoleum table. His eyes were wide and his bushy black hair, dried by the sun, stood up wildly. He was rested and I could tell he was excited as he wolfed down a doughnut we'd bought in town the night before. "Five? And they were about three pounds? Why didn't you keep them? I'd have kept them. Every one of them."

"All the men were getting good fish," I said.

"Why didn't you wake me?"

"I tried to, old man, but you wouldn't be woke."

"Want to go back out? Do you think I can get a couple? Everyone was getting them? How many fish did you actually see caught?"

"Whenever you're ready we'll go out," I said, smiling.

"You're sure I can get some? They're in the channel, like the manager said they'd be this week?"

"Let's find out," I said.

The lake was crowded now. As I moved the boat out of the springs and into the channel, I could see at once that the Glory Hole now had eight or ten boats anchored in or near it. The sun had burned off the mist and the rain had stopped; it was late morning, and I could see down into the water, right to the bottom in the areas that didn't have weeds. It was a shallow lake, and not particularly clear, and in the summer the weeds grew thick and high. I saw several large fish swimming slowly along the bottom and cut the motor. The boy looked over the side as we circled back, and he saw them too. They were large brook trout—four or five pounds apiece.

"Did you see them, Dad?" he asked. "Did you see the size of them?"

"I saw."

"Shall we fish here?"

"Let's head farther out," I said. "Near where I got them this morning."

We headed out toward the hole, but several boats were anchored where I had been. I did not want to fish too close to them. I wished there were no other boats on the lake.

Finally, we cut the motor at the edge of the weeds, where the hold abruptly ended. I told the boy to cast in toward the other boats. His rod was rigged, and he began to cast before I'd fully lowered the anchor chain. He drew the lure back quickly, with the rod tip held high and steady. He made four casts this way; I watched him while I tied on another leech and checked my leader for frays.

"Put the rod tip down and bring the lure back in short jerks," I said. "You're bringing it back too fast."

"Like this?" he asked, and lowered the rod and brought the lure back even faster, still without the short jerks that had worked so well for me sixteen years earlier.

"No, no," I said. "Slower. Slower."

One of the men in my morning spot had hooked another fish on a fly rod, and he fought in noisily, with Texas howls. The boy looked over and then began to reel his lure in fast again.

In a few minutes another man had a fish on his fly rod, and then another rod bent in that high curving arc, too. I began to cast now, from the bow of our boat, and on the third cast hooked a solid cutthroat.

"This spinning rod is no good," the boy said.

"It will catch more and bigger fish than a fly," I told him.

"That's what you said while we were driving here. All the way across the country you told me I'd have no trouble catching fish with a spinning rod. I haven't gotten a thing. Not a strike."

I put my rod down and took his spinning rod. It was a strange weapon in my hands. I had not used one in many years. I had stopped using a spinning rod after I'd fished this lake the last time, and I had gone through a long apprentice-ship learning the magic of a fly rod. I had caught nothing for a long time, and then suddenly the line no longer whipped down on the water be-hind me, and the fly no longer slapped down on the water, and my distance grew from twenty to forty and then maybe sixty-five feet.

I flicked the metal lure far out into the hole and let it sink, and then brought it back in short, sharp jerks. I cast three or four more times, drew the lure back with those slow, sharp jerks, and then handed the rod to the boy. He cast again, and then again. He imparted a better motion to the lure now, but he still caught no fish. The other men took three more fish on their fly rods.

I cast again, and then again. On the fourth cast I hooked another cutthroat; he splashed at the surface several times, and then came in with-

out difficulty.

"I can't get a thing," the boy said. "I'm just no good at it. I'll never catch anything."

"You will. I'm sure you will."

"You've been saying that."

"Try a few more casts," I coached.

"Why?"

"You can't catch anything if you don't cast."

The sun was bright and hot now, and many of the boats were beginning to head back to the dock. I pulled the anchor and headed closer to the center of the hole.

But when we'd anchored in the new spot and he'd cast four or five more times, he gave it up and sat down.

"How long are we going to stay here?" he asked.

"We can go back now," I said. "I only wanted you to get a couple of fish."

"I haven't caught any," he said.

"I know," I said.

"Look, Dad," he said. "I like fishing, I really do. And I like being out here with you. But I can't catch anything on this spinning rod. Maybe if I knew how to use a fly rod it would be different. But I don't. And I don't have the same kind of patience you have. I like fishing, but I don't like not catching anything. You don't care. You really don't. But I do. And I'm not going to get any. Not today. Not tomorrow. Not any day this week. I know I won't."

"Well," I said, scratching my head, "why don't you try twenty more casts, and if you don't get one we'll head back to the cabin and maybe visit Virginia City or the Park this after-noon." Perhaps we should head back at once, I thought. I had enjoyed being on the lake alone at daybreak—catching some fish, losing the big fish. Perhaps it had been a mistake to come back to this lake with the boy. He would have enjoyed the beach more, and I wouldn't have wanted to fish so much. I never seemed to fish enough but it mattered much less when there were no trout nearby.

The boy began casting and counting, bringing in the lure much too fast. Thirteen, fourteen, fifteen. Nothing. Sixteen. Nothing.

On the seventeenth cast, the little glass rod jerked down in a sharp arc. A good fish. A very good fish.

"Good grief!" he shouted. "Can't hold him!"

"Let him have line," I shouted back. "Don't force him. Keep your rod tip high. It's a good fish, a very good fish."

The fish moved steadily from the boat. I could tell by the way the line throbbed slowly that it was a substantial fish, a brookie, I thought.

The boy lowered the rod tip and I leaned over to lift it up. The boat swayed and I never reached the rod, but the boy smiled broadly and raised the rod so that the full force of the bend could work against the fish.

Don't lose it. For godsake don't lose it, I thought.

"He's still taking line, Dad. I can't stop him."

"He'll turn," I said. "He's got to turn in a minute or two. Don't force him. Don't let him get into the weeds, but don't force him. Don't drop that rod tip!"

The line went slack.

"No. No!" I said.

"Have I lost him? No. I can't have lost him."

"Reel quickly," I said. "Maybe he's turned. Maybe he's still there."

"He's there," the boy shouted. "I can feel him. Good grief, he's big. Can you see him yet?

I won't lose him now."

I looked over where the line entered the water. I strained to see the fish, but could not. It had to be a big brookie.

Now the fish was angling off to the left. He might go completely around the boat. As the line came toward me, I lifted it and let it pass over my head; for a second I could feel the big fish throbbing at the other end of the line. The fish came around the front of the boat and the boy fought him on the other side.

We both saw it at the same time. A huge male brookie. We saw it twisting and shaking ten feet below the surface, the silver lure snug in the corner of its mouth.

"It's huge. It's the biggest brookie I've ever seen."

"I'm not going to lose him," the boy said. "I can't lose it now."

"You won't lose it. He's well hooked. He's too high and too tired to get into the weeds. You've got him beat, son. I'll get the net." I looked under the seat and came up with the little teardrop stream net.

"He'll never fit," the boy said. "He'll never fit in that—whooooa. He's taking line again. He's going around the other side of the boat now."

The fish was close to the boat but not yet beaten. He went deep and around the corner of the boat. I watched for the line to angle out, on the other side of the boat. It never did.

"The anchor chain!" I shouted. "Don't let him get in the anchor chain."

"I can't feel him," said the boy. "The line's on something but I can't feel the fish fighting anymore."

I scurried the length of the boat, bent under the rod, and then lowered myself where the anchor chain entered the water. At first I could see nothing. But then I saw it. The huge brook trout was still on the line; I could see it five feet down, the silver lure still in the corner of its mouth. He was circling slowly around the anchor chain, and I could see that the line was already wound six or seven times around the links. It would not come free. Not ever.

"Is it there?" the boy called. "Is it still there?"

"You're going to lose him, son. He's in the anchor chain. There's no way I can get it free."

"Oh, no, no," he said.

I put my nose down to the surface of the water. The fish had gone around the chain twice more, and his distance from the chain was growing smaller and smaller. It kept circling, slowly, every now and then jerking it head back against the tug of the line.

"I can't lose him! I can't," the boy said.

"There's nothing to be done. If I lift the chain, he'll break off; if I leave him, he'll pull out in another couple of turns."

"What about the net?"

"Don't think I can reach him."

"Try, Dad. Please try. I can't lose this fish. Not this one."

I took the little stream net and dipped it far down. The cold water stung my raw hands, and the net came short by more than a foot. The fish made a lunge and I was sure it would break free.

"Got him?"

"Nope. Too far down. Can't reach him."

"Maybe someone with one of the boat nets . . ." But he stopped. The other boats were gone from the lake; we had the Glory Hole to ourselves.

The fish went around the rope again. There was only a foot and a half between him and the chain now. The big brookie was tired. It was half on its side.

I took the boy's arm and pulled him down to where I knelt. It didn't matter if he let the line go slack now. Together we pushed our faces close to the surface of the water and peered down. In the liquid below us, we looked through the reflections of both our faces, side by side, overlapping and rippled, and saw the huge fish.

I reached again, pressing the net down through the water as carefully as I could, trying hard not to frighten it again. My arm was in up to my shoulder and I felt the cold lake water slosh onto my chest. The fish came a little higher this time. I could almost touch it with the end of the net—and I saw clearly now that even if I could get near enough to it, the fish was far too big for the little net, and the lure was almost torn out. There was no chance.

"You'll never get him, Dad," the boy said.

He was holding onto my shoulder now with his left arm, and looking constantly through our reflections at the shadow that was his fish.

"It's lost," I whispered.

And then the fish floated up five or six inches, I pressed the net toward its head, felt cold water on my face, saw the head of the huge fish go into the net, saw the line break behind the lure, and lifted madly.

A year has passed, and the etching remains, as if fixed by acid in steelplate: our faces in the water, merged; the tremendous circling trout; the fish half in and half out of that tiny teardrop net, and then the two of us, side by side in the bottom of that aluminum boat, our raw hands clutching a thing bright sliver gray and mottled, and laughing as if we were four days drunk.

[excerpt]

166 Friends on the Water

Tewnty-One Beats Twenty by Thomas McGuane

Sea trout are enigmatic fish to say the least. They are brown trout and therefore subject to that species' notorious moodiness. Sea trout have elicited compulsive fly-changing, night-fishing, pool-stoning, and belly-crawling extremes from their devotees. The sea-run version brings an oceanic rapacity to the smaller world of the river, but they are no easier to understand. We flew into Ciudad Rio Grande in Tierra del Fuego for the promise of favorable full-moon tides. We hoped they would send us fresh waves of such fish.

Our host, Estevan, was by now our old friend. Stevie loved to fish, knew his river well, and kept us amused by his detached sense of humor wherein anglers and all their passions were seen with the objectivity of a good researcher closeted with a houseful of laboratory mice. If one party returned with six fish while another returned with four, Stevie would note, "Six beats four." This later took on a life of its own and Stevie was heard to say, "Eighty-one beats eighty," without any explanation as to what this referred to—

though it had to be something other than fish.

His car is a low mountain of caked Tierra del Fuego mud, rod racks on top, rap tapes on the front seat, and a United Colors of Benetton sticker in the rear window. We rumble across the grasslands to the deep, throbbing beat of the Fugees ordering Chinese food in a New York restaurant, sheep fleeing before us in flocks, condor shadows racing from the Andes. Stevie looks around, takes it all in. "Thirty-seven beats twenty-nine."

Yvon believes in going deep. I only go deep when I am utterly discouraged. When Yvon notices me reacting to the sight of his four-hundred-grain shooting head landing on the surface of the Rio Grande like a lead cobra, he states, "To save the river, first I must destroy it." This Pol Pot—style remark fires my determination.

He gets into a pod of bright sea trout and catches one after another with devastating efficiency. Some yards above him, I hold a cold stick, consoling myself despite the cries of my success-gorged partner, "I feel like a shrimper!" The fish

must have been running, their silvery rolls and huge boils increasing. At last, I begin hooking up. They are beyond big. They are heavy and violent, taking the fly with malevolence. We are so far into the zone that not even approaching night can drive us out.

A kind of hypnosis results from the long hours of staring into this grasslands river, trying to comprehend its ocean-run fish. I put on a small bomber and begin working the far grassy bank, enjoying the provocative wake the fly pulls behind it. Suddenly, a fish runs my fly down, making an eight-foot rip in the silky flow of the river. I can feel this one well down into the cork of my double-hander. The fight takes us up and down the pool, and the weight I perceive at the end of my line keeps me on edge. Several times I think I have the fish landed, only to have it power out of the shallows.

In the end, Stevie netted the fish. "Look at those shoulders," he said. We weighed her in the net and Yvon came up for a look; a twenty-five-pound female. To judge by her brilliant silver color and sharp black spots, she was just out of the ocean. Releasing her, I never imagined such a trout belly would ever hang between my two hands. As she swam off the shelf, she pulled a three-foot bow wake. In the sea yesterday, she was going up to the mountains. We watched her go.

Yvon noted that with twenty-one sea-run brown trout, nineteen over fifteen pounds, we had just had the best fishing day we would ever have. We were tired and vaguely stunned. There was almost the sense that wherever we had been going as trout fishermen we had just gotten there. Stevie thought about it all, let his eye follow a flight of ashy-headed geese passing overhead, and said, "Twenty-one beats twenty."

The truth is, fish have very little sex life.
If you have ever tried to make love under water, you will know why.

—ED ZERN, *HOW TO TELL FISH FROM FISHERMEN*

O Come All Ye Old Faithful by Pat Straub

I pour a little rum in my cider and get typing. At present, I am coupled with winter, 400 square feet of cabin, a half-empty bottle of rum, and memories of my rookie year of guiding in Yellowstone Park. The only sound breaking the tap-tap of the 'writer is the occasional gust of wind dusting off the roof. A summer spent on the firehole seems so distant now. Far off like the bonefish flats and snook mangroves of someplace tropical that I'm too poor to visit.

After growing up in Montana and then four years of college in Wisconsin, I was ready to return and grace the rivers and fly shops with my talents as a fly-fishing expert. In the first month of guiding I got skunked, removed embedded hooks, played marriage counselor, learned Happy is also a 300-pounder from Texas as well as an emotion, landed an SUV, and got used for my body, which wasn't too bad now that I think about it.

The girl had come out to Montana with her dad on a week's fishing trip. After three days of fishing and early nights in The Park, she wanted to sample Bozeman's bar scene. We got off the firehole early, drove the canyon from West picking out sweet trout lies on the Gallatin, and arrived in the Bozone just as the sun set behind the Tabacco

Roots. The Bridgers were lit in gold light, sort of like a fresh tap of pale ale. To bring this one in quickly, we hit some bars and headed to a buddy's house and were stuck with sharing the same room, and in that room, the same queen-sized bed.

PMD's had been the hatch on the firehole, which means July, which means hot. She was in panties and a tank top, I had on sport shorts and a tee. While I was reading the latest LaFontaine article she rolled over and said to me, "Wanna wrestle?" No kidding. Five minutes into our bout, shirts are on the floor and I'm hoping the other half is next, when she says, "Wanna see my tattoo?" There goes the second half, as Victoria's Secret lets fly and reveals a butterfly with wings spread, almost like a Hexagena hatching. Soon she has me pinned against the bed and I feel her shake, she moans, and then collapses onto my chest. Through strands of her salty hair I stared at paint peeling on the ceiling, thinking, "What about me?"

I guided her and her dad two more days in The Park. Pops tipped me pretty well and they booked for the following year. At that moment I knew I was destined to be a guide: self-sacrifice for the benefit of the client—and repeat business.

Opening Day by Jon Wurtmann

In my childhood the wait until Opening Day was torturous, as it was always the third Saturday in April. In southern Connecticut the snow was long gone, and the fragrant, loamy soil yielded crocus, hyacinth, and tulips. With spring so clearly in evidence, the legality of some arbitrary future date put a mighty burden on a young boy. Finally, Opening Day eve would roll around, and we'd ready our gear, lay out our clothes for our pre-dawn march, and then dig for night-crawlers. Exhausted with excitement, we'd crawl under the covers and reread every *Field & Stream* and *Outdoor Life* in the house, by the covert beams of our flashlights.

My father would rouse us up in the dark, and we'd spring from the sack into our flannel shirts and dungarees. We always walked to the little town center, even though it was a mile distant. Somehow, the walk became part of the tradition, and you don't question tradition when luck is involved with your ultimate quest. We'd pass the stately, iconic Congregational church, white clapboard and wavy glass dating back two centuries, then past the little playhouse, and across the bridge where we'd peer down intently into the steel gray waters looking for a hint of life. A flick of a tail, the dart of a young fish, the telltale rise of a feeding trout.

Beyond the bridge, the stream broke over a rock ledge and tumbled into a large waterfall. As mesmerizing as the roar and the spray was, the fact that someone had built a house halfway down the steep side was even more amazing to us. Old man Merwin lived there. Revered by us kids as a fly tier and photographer, he was our resident Ansel Adams, John Muir, and Henry David Thoreau rolled into one. And he lived right by the side of a waterfall!

As the noise of the falls faded behind us, we quickened our pace down Lover's Lane—still quite a mystery to us—toward the Norwalk River.

At this point the road turned into dirt tracks, rutted and potholed. We hushed ourselves as we entered the woods here—half from fear, half from reverence. The river gurgled through the screen of early green buds, fiddleheads, and skunk cabbage. The air ticked down a few degrees and held a damp chill as the track ended at the old train station, now abandoned, windows gone, seemingly out of place in these deep woods where once a thriving depot stood. It looked forlorn with its empty eyes, rimmed white in the peeling red siding. It was a creepy and holy place for us; a memento mori of lives past. It was also the site of the dam, a six-foot-high spillway that created a pond upstream, and a dangerous, turbulent deep hole below. A fishing hole.

We'd choose just the right night-crawlers— not too big—and drop them into the roaring foam backwash. Without bobbers, which were useless in this maelstrom, we'd fish by feel, keeping a tight line—inasmuch as the attention span of a boy allows—and intuit the subtle bite of the trout.

In later years, during the runoff, foolish boys would challenge this river, and sometimes the dam. Some of us would make it out alive, some would not. I was nearly drowned by a huge sweeper: a fallen maple whose trunk snapped my canoe neatly in half, then held me underwater, and whose branches ensnarled my friend as he swept beneath it. We both emerged badly shaken, without our boat, but alive. Others attempted the dam, and were trapped in the vortex beneath it. We'd learn a deep respect for this river and its ability to take what is most precious.

But on Opening Day, the river gave up its treasures to anxious little boys. Standing safely on the bank, we caught our shimmering childhood trophies: brilliant speckled trout, smelling richly of the stream, of spring, of life.

Sam, Tam, and Jazz by Tony Orman

When you've fished with a companion for a decade or more, rarely missing a fishing trip, it comes as a sad moment when you realize there will be no more. It was like that thirteen years ago, when Sam departed. Sam was actually a female, a rich golden-colored Labrador.

Her replacement, Tam, proved a great fishing friend too, but, of course, with a different personality. Now her life has drawn to a close and I have only memories of her ways and fishing companionship. But the memories of fishing with them both are sweet and indelible . . .

I remember Sam's first outing after trout, one warm November evening on the Tukituki River. I had hooked a fish, a fat three-pound rainbow, and Sam, just a youngster, was startled and curious and then finally downright inquisitive. She jumped into the water with the trout in the shallows—a flurry of four delinquent canine legs tangled with the nylon leader and sploshing trout—and the tippet parted. Sam was mystified. The trout had gone. For an instant I was annoyed and then that melted at the comical sight of the puzzled Labrador youngster.

Sam became a controlled but eager fishing companion. Before age dimmed and then extinguished her eyesight, she would spot cruising trout in the gin-clear pools and watch them intently, showing admirable self-control and indicating her inward excitement only by the quivering of her tail.

Sam made mistakes, particularly as a puppy. Just a few months old, she showed a liking for anything connected with fishing by gnawing a gaping hole in a pair of waders that I had carelessly left lying in the carport.

One evening, again on the Tukituki River, I was in the middle of tying on a nymph, tightening the knot in my teeth, when Sam blundered in, got her leg around the line and tightened the nymph into my lip with as neat a timing as any angler could hope for! I was literally hooked!

We enjoyed so many fishing trips. Different rivers, sometimes an evening visit to a river, other times a full weekend during which we walked miles into the mountains where the rivers ran crystal clear, where deer grazed the river flats at first light and the ridges towered above us.

Sam knew when a trip was in the offing. Any move with a fishing rod was a signal to make her way quietly to the car—if the door was open, she would unobtrusively seat herself inside and patiently wait. Just donning a pair of old corduroy trousers that I might wear fishing, generated eager interest in her.

Tam was an ideal trout-fishing companion too.

Like Sam she was a honey golden brown. She too showed a natural aptitude for fishing right from puppy days. As a wee mite of a puppy, one day she disappeared. We were mystified and spent an hour frantically searching outside until eventually we discovered her sound asleep behind a bedroom door—significantly, she was on my fishing vest and shirt!

Dogs are so loyal—even if they could talk they would not betray some "secret" wilderness fishing spot—they are so sincere and genuine. I have had human fishing companions return to places I have shown them, and ruthlessly fish them with the emphasis on killing. I quickly learned my lesson and took to fishing alone on most occasions. I was alone but never lonely, for Tam or Sam was usually there.

I will always remember one trip Tam and I did that was sheer magic. Together we walked up into the mountains, fishing upstream using the nymph, spotting trout first and then stalking and casting to them. The trout were in fine feeding fettle, coming to any well-presented nymph with eagerness. I remember the trout but recall more vividly the beautiful mountain valley, the sunlight catching the bounce of the rapids as I lay back on a grassy river flat and dozed in the warm sunshine. But equally I remember the companionship of Tam . . . her love of the water as we crossed, her absorption in bringing a trout to the net, her patience as I dallied, and a host of other loyal traits.

Come to think of it, a Labrador is a model fishing companion, something all of us could aspire to be.

Often in the back country I would combine deer hunting with trout fishing. I remember, with Sam, hunting a North Island valley that had a good trout river in it. In my pack I had stowed a "backpacker" fly rod.

Our hunting took us in a big circle until we found ourselves in the river several miles downstream. We walked up river, fishing, knowing that our route would lead us back to the car. Gradually the valley sides hemmed in and the river crossings became deeper and swifter. Then we came to a deep, dark pool hemmed in by rock faces. From somewhere around the bend came the rumbling roar of rapids. It was impossible to get through.

With daylight running out, I backtracked downstream searching the steep walls until I spotted a series of steps and began to pull myself up. For Sam it was impossible, so I had to help her. At each step I pushed her ahead and then hauled myself up—each time Sam gave me exuberant licks of gratitude for my assistance. Eventually we climbed our way out of the canyon, and rested at the top with a great sense of relief.

Such experiences, and shared fun fishing, build a strong bond between man and dog. It gets deeper and, when the time comes, the parting is so wrenching.

Rudyard Kipling warned: "Brothers and sisters, I bid you beware, of giving your heart to a dog to tear."

It is true, but there are undeniably rich rewards and warm memories of the times spent together outdoors by man and dog.

So it's not surprising that now that Tam has departed, I have a new companion—Jazz, short for Jasmine. Cream and stocky of build, she is sensitive with a perceptive nature. I only have to pick up my fly rod or fly-fishing jacket, and she waits by the car with tail wagging. There are many great trips ahead for the two of us, together!

Fly fishing is solitary, contemplative, misanthropic, scientific in some hands,
poetic in others, and laced with conflicting aesthetic considerations.
It is not even clear if catching fish is actually the point.

—John Gierach, *Dances with Trout*

To the Fisher Fishing Alone by Seth Norman

Much of the romance in fly fishing emerges from the image of a fisher alone. Limned against a rush of moving water or tree-broken sky, testing the elements in a game both physical and mental—no audience is necessary or even welcome. There's only room for two at the ends of a line.

Paradoxically enough, there's another tradition of fishers sharing on a bank or by a fire, maybe while driving home into a night illuminated by headlights and the pastel glows of the dashboard, the passion of pursuit.

I've fished alone for tens of thousands of hours now, days, even weeks at a time. I do not remember a moment of loneliness.

I also spent twelve years fishing with the same partner and am a better angler for it, maybe a better man; unquestionably richer by far. Part of the reason comes from the curious fact that, for me, under certain circumstances, fishing can be one of the best partner sports.

{excerpt}

I learned long ago that although fish do make a difference—the difference in angling—catching them does not; so that he who is content to not-catch fish in the most skillful and refined manner will have his time and attention free for the accumulation of a thousand experiences, the memory of which will remain for his enjoyment long after any recollection of fish would have faded.

—Sparse Grey Hackle

Story Index

Author Index

Source Notes

8: From Tully Stroud, *The Trout Chaser's Journal* (San Francisco: Chronicle Books, 1986). Used with permission of Chronicle Books LLC, San Francisco.

10: © Jerry Darkes, by permission of the author.

16: From Nick Lyons, *Spring Creek* (New York: Atlantic Monthly Press, 1992). Used by permission of Grove/Atlantic, Inc.

24: Reprinted from *Eastern Fly Fishing*, Spring 2006, by permission of the author.

28: Reprinted from *The Drake*, 2003, by permission of the author.

32: From *The Armchair Angler*, ed. Terry Brykcznski and David Reuther (New York: Scribner's, 1986).

36, 74: © Bob White, by permission of the author.

42: From *The Field & Stream Treasury of Trout Fishing*, ed. Leonard M. Wright (Guilford, CT: The Lyons Press, 2004). Copyright © 2001 by Times Mirror Magazine. Used by permission of The Lyons Press, Guilford, CT.

44: From Robert Traver, *Trout Madness* (New York: St. Martin's Press, 1960), by permission of the publisher.

48: From *Seasons of the Angler: A Fisherman's Anthology*, ed. David Seybold (New York: Weidenfeld & Nicolson, 1988).

56: From Norman Maclean, *A River Runs Through It* (Chicago: University of Chicago Press, 1989), by permission of the publisher.

60, 106: © Chris Santella, by permission of the author.

62, 186: From Seth Norman, *Meanderings of a Fly Fisherman* (Belgrade, MT: Wilderness Adventures Press, 1996), by permission of the author.

66: Reprinted from *Fly Fish America*, 2002, by permission of the author.

70, 94, 118, 180: From *Short Casts: A Collection of Fly Fishing Stories from Australia and New Zealand*, ed. Rob Sloane (Richmond, Australia: FlyLife, 2004), by permission of the respective authors.

82: From Steve Chapple, *Confessions of an Eco-Redneck* (Cambridge, MA: Da Capo Press, 2001).

84, 176: © Jon Wurtmann, by permission of the author.

98: From *Headwaters: Montana Writers on Water and Wilderness*, ed. Annick Smith (Missoula, MT: Hellgate Writers, 1996), by permission of the author.

104: Reprinted from *The Drake*, 2002, by permission of the author.

108: From *Seasons of the Angler: A Fisherman's Anthology*, ed. David Seybold (New York: Weidenfeld & Nicolson, 1988), by permission of the author.

122: Reprinted from *Fly Fisherman*, Late Season 1979, by permission of the author.

128: From Lyla Foggia, *Reel Women: The World of Women Who Fish* (Hillsboro, England: Beyond Words, 1995), by permission of the publisher.

132: From Margot Page, *Little Rivers* (New York: Avon Books, 1995), by permission of the author.

136: Reprinted from *The Drake*, 2005, by permission of the author.

138: From Bob Ripley, *Jungle Trout and Other Streamside Stories* (Marietta, NY: Jungle Trout, 2005), by permission of the author.

142: From John Gierach, *The View from Rat Lake* (Boulder, CO: Pruett Publishing, 1988), by permission of the author.

150: Originally published in *Forbes FYI*, May 10, 1993, and in this form in *A Different Angle: Fly Fishing Stories by Women*, ed. Holly Morris (Berkeley, CA: Seal Press, 1995). © 1995 by Holly Morris. Reprinted by permission of the author.

152: From John England, *Black Gnat* (Christchurch, New Zealand: Caxton Press, 1990), by permission of the author.

156: From Ernest Schwiebert, *Remembrance of Rivers Past* (London: Macmillan Co., 1972), by permission of Erik Schwiebert.

160: From Nick Lyons, *Fishing Widows* (New York: Simon & Schuster, 1989), by permission of the author.

170: From *Patagonia: Notes from the Field*, ed. Nora Gallagher (San Francisco: Chronicle Books, 1999), by permission of the author.

174: Reprinted from *The Drake*, 2002, by permission of Pat Straub/Montana Fishing Outfitters, Helena, MT.

Acknowledgments

The author would like to thank the following people and organizations for helping to make this book possible: Frontiers International Travel, for their generosity and for providing the opportunity to visit many of these wonderful destinations; Susan Rockrise, my partner in life, for her many creative ideas and her support; The Orvis Company, for their ongoing commitment to good photography; Jennifer Levesque and Kate Norment, my editors, for their insight and good judgment; and the many friends and fishing guides without whom I couldn't have managed.

Published in 2007 by Stewart, Tabori & Chang
An imprint of Harry N. Abrams, Inc.

Photographs copyright © 2007 by R. Valentine Atkinson
For text permissions, see page 191.

Library of Congress Cataloging-in-Publication Data
Atkinson, R. Valentine.
  Friends on the water : fly fishing in good company / photographs by R. Valentine Atkinson.
    p. cm.
  Includes index.
  ISBN-13: 978-1-58479-573-5
  ISBN-10: 1-58479-573-5
  1.   Fly fishing—Anecdotes. 2. Atkinson, R. Valentine. I. Title.

SH456.A85 2006
799.12'4—dc22

2006028412

Editor: Jennifer Levesque
Designers: Julie Hoffer and Nancy Leonard
Production Manager: Jacquie Poirier

The text of this book was composed in Goudy Village and Monoline Script.

Printed and bound in the United States of America
10 9 8 7 6 5 4 3 2 1

harry n. abrams, inc.
a subsidiary of La Martinière Groupe

115 West 18th Street
New York, NY 10011
www.hnabooks.com